America's
Founding Fathers

America's Founding Fathers

Their Uncommon Wisdom and Wit

Edited by Bill Adler

ROWMAN & LITTLEFIELD
Lanham • Boulder • New York • London

Published by Rowman & Littlefield
A wholly owned subsidiary of The Rowman & Littlefield Publishing Group, Inc.
4501 Forbes Boulevard, Suite 200, Lanham, Maryland 20706
www.rowman.com

Unit A, Whitacre Mews, 26-34 Stannary Street, London SE11 4AB, United Kingdom

Distributed by NATIONAL BOOK NETWORK

British Library Cataloguing in Publication Information Available

Library of Congress Cataloging-in-Publication Data
The hardback edition of this book was previously catalogued by the Library of Congress
as follows:

America's founding fathers : their uncommon wisdom and wit / [compiled by] Bill Adler.
  p. cm.
  Includes index.
  1. Statesmen—United States—Quotations. 2. Presidents—United States—Quotations. 3.
United States—Politics and government—1783–1809—Quotations, maxims, etc. 4.
United States—Politics and government—1775–1783—Quotations, maxims, etc.
I. Adler, Bill, 1956–2014

E302.5 .A47 2003
973.4'092'2—dc21   2002014503

ISBN 0-87833-284-7 (cloth : alk. paper)
ISBN 978-1-4422-3935-7 (pbk. : alk. paper)
ISBN 978-1-4616-2521-6 (ebook)

CONTENTS

Contents

ACKNOWLEDGMENT

The Author wishes to thank Tom Steele for his research assistance.

INTRODUCTION: THE FOUNDING FATHERS— A BRIEF OVERVIEW

The fifty-five delegates who attended the Constitutional Convention were a distinguished body of men who represented a cross-section of eighteenth-century American leadership. According to the National Archives and Records Administration, almost all of them were well-educated men of means who were dominant in their communities and states, and many were also prominent in national affairs. Virtually every one had taken part in the Revolution; at least twenty-nine had served in the Continental forces, most of them in positions of command.

The group, as a whole, had extensive political experience. At the time of the convention, four-fifths, or forty-one individuals, were or had been members of the Continental Congress.

The delegates practiced a wide range of occupations, and many men pursued more than one career simultaneously. Thirty-five were lawyers or had benefited from legal training, though not all of them relied on the profession for a livelihood. Some had also become judges.

At the time of the convention, thirteen individuals were businessmen, merchants, or shippers. Six were major land speculators. Eleven speculated in securities on a large scale. Twelve owned or managed slave-operated plantations or large farms. James Madison also owned slaves.

Nine of the men received a substantial part of their income from public office. Three had retired from active economic endeavors. Franklin was a scientist, in addition to his other activities. Three were physicians, and one was a university president. One had been a minister.

A few of the delegates were wealthy. George Washington and Robert Morris ranked among the nation's most prosperous men. Four others were also extremely well to do. Most of the others had financial resources that ranged from good to excellent. Seven had somewhat straitened circumstances, though they all managed to live comfortably.

A considerable number of the men were born into leading families; others, including Benjamin Franklin and Alexander

Hamilton, were self-made men who had risen from humble beginnings.

Most of the delegates were natives of the thirteen colonies. In fact, only eight were born elsewhere. Reflecting the mobility that has always characterized American life, many of them had moved from one state to another. Sixteen individuals had already lived or worked in more than one state or colony. Several others had studied or traveled abroad.

The educational background of the Founding Fathers was diverse. Some, like Franklin, were largely self-taught and had received scant formal training. Others had obtained instruction from private tutors or at academies. About half of the individuals had attended or graduated from college in the British North American colonies or abroad. Some men held advanced and honorary degrees. For the most part, the delegates were a well-educated group.

For their era, the delegates to the convention (like the signers of the Declaration of Independence) were remarkably long-lived. Their average age at death was almost sixty-seven.

Most of the delegates married and raised children. At least nine married more than once. Four were lifelong bachelors. In terms of religious affiliation, the men mirrored the overwhelmingly Protestant character of American religious life at the time and were members of various denominations. Only two were Roman Catholics.

The delegates' subsequent careers reflected their abilities as well as the vagaries of fate. Most were successful, although seven suffered serious financial reverses that left them in or near bankruptcy. Two were involved in possibly treasonous activities. Yet, as they had done before the convention, most of the group continued to render outstanding public service, particularly to the new government they had helped to create.

Many delegates held important state positions, including governor and legislator. And most of the delegates contributed in many ways to the cultural life of their cities, communities, and states. Not surprisingly, many of their sons and other descendants were to occupy high positions in American political and intellectual life.

Our focus in this volume is on the words of the most distinguished of the Founding Fathers, on how these extraordinary men felt about their country, families, communities, religion, culture, economics, education, and life in general.

—BILL ADLER
New York, New York
December 2003

BENJAMIN FRANKLIN

(1706–1790)

Scientist, Diplomat, and Writer

"If you would not be forgotten as soon as you are dead and rotten, either write things worth reading or do things worth the writing."

"Be in general virtuous, and you will be happy."

"The great secret of succeeding in conversation is to admire little, to hear much; always to distrust our own reason, and sometimes that of our friends; never to pretend to wit, but to make that of others appear as much as possibly we can; to hearken to what is said and to answer to the purpose."

"There never was a good war nor a bad peace."

"Remember, that time is money."

"A benevolent man should allow a few faults in himself, to keep his friends in countenance."

"I should have no objection to go over the same life from its beginning to the end: requesting only the advantage authors have, of correcting in a second edition the faults of the first."

"Our new Constitution is now established, and has an appearance that promises permanency; but in this world nothing can be said to be certain, except *death* and *taxes*."

"We must indeed all hang together, or, most assuredly, we shall all hang separately."

"The way to see by faith is to shut the eye of reason."

"I cannot conceive otherwise than that He, the Infinite Father, expects or requires no worship or praise from us, but that He is even infinitely above it."

"When a religion is good, I conceive it will support itself; and when it does not support itself, and God does not take care to support it so that its professors are obliged to call for help of the civil power, 'tis a sign, I apprehend, of its being a bad one."

"I think vital religion has always suffered when orthodoxy is more regarded than virtue. The scriptures assure me that on the last day we shall not be examined on what we thought but what we did."

"Lighthouses are more helpful than churches."

"If we look back into history for the character of the present sects of Christianity, we shall find few that have not in turns been persecutors, and complainers of persecution. The primitive Christians thought persecution extremely wrong in Pagans, but practiced it on one another. The first Protestants of the Church of England blamed persecution in the Romish church, but practiced it on the Puritans. They found it wrong in Bishops, but fell into the practice both here (England) and in New England."

"Those who would give up essential Liberty, to purchase a little temporary Safety, deserve neither Liberty nor Safety."

Franklin on John Adams: "Always an honest man, often a great one—but sometimes absolutely mad."

"No nation was ever ruined by trade."

"Idleness and pride tax with a heavier hand than kings and parliaments. If we can get rid of the former, we may easily bear the latter."

THE RATTLESNAKE AS A SYMBOL OF AMERICA

The following letter appeared in the *Pennsylvania Journal* on December 27, 1775. It was signed by "An American

Guesser," who was recently identified as Benjamin Franklin. Written between the time the American Revolution got underway, but still before the Declaration of Independence was signed, it offers quite a unique glimpse into the workings of Franklin's observant mind.

"I observed on one of the drums belonging to the marines now raising, there was painted a Rattle-Snake, with this modest motto under it, 'Don't tread on me.' As I know it is the custom to have some device on the arms of every country, I supposed this may have been intended for the arms of America; and as I have nothing to do with public affairs, and as my time is perfectly my own, in order to divert an idle hour, I sat down to guess what could have been intended by this uncommon device—I took care, however, to consult on this occasion a person who is acquainted with heraldry, from whom I learned, that it is a rule among the learned of that science 'That the worthy properties of the animal, in the crest-born, shall be considered,' and, 'That the base ones cannot have been intended'; he likewise informed me that the ancients considered the serpent as an emblem of wisdom, and in a certain attitude of endless duration—both which circumstances I suppose may have been had in view. Having gained this intelligence, and recollecting that countries are sometimes represented by animals peculiar to them, it occurred to me that the Rattle-Snake is found in no other quarter of the world besides America, and may therefore have been chosen, on that account, to represent her.

"But then 'the worthy properties' of a Snake I judged would be hard to point out. This rather raised than suppressed my curiosity, and having frequently seen the Rattle-Snake, I ran over in my mind every property by which she was distinguished, not only from other animals, but from those of the same genus or class of animals, endeavoring to fix some meaning to each, not wholly inconsistent with common sense.

"I recollected that her eye excelled in brightness, that of any other animal, and that she has no eye-lids. She may therefore be esteemed an emblem of vigilance. She never begins an attack, nor, when once engaged, ever surrenders: She is therefore an emblem of magnanimity and true courage. As if anxious to prevent all pretensions of quarreling with her, the weapons with which nature has furnished her, she conceals in the roof of her mouth, so that, to those who are unacquainted with her, she appears to be a most defenseless animal; and even when those weapons are shown and extended for her defense, they appear weak and contemptible; but their wounds however small, are decisive and fatal. Conscious of this, she never wounds 'till she has generously given notice, even to her enemy, and cautioned him against the danger of treading on her.

"Was I wrong, Sir, in thinking this a strong picture of the temper and conduct of America? The poison of her teeth is the necessary means of digesting her food, and at the same time is certain destruction to her enemies. This may be understood to intimate that those things which are destructive to our enemies, may be to us not only harmless, but absolutely necessary to our existence. I confess I was wholly at a loss what to make of the rattles, 'till I went back and counted them and found them just thirteen, exactly the number of the Colonies united in America; and I recollected too that this was the only part of the Snake which increased in numbers. Perhaps it might be only fancy, but, I conceited the painter had shown a half formed additional rattle, which, I suppose, may have been intended to represent the province of Canada.

"'Tis curious and amazing to observe how distinct and independent of each other the rattles of this animal are, and yet how firmly they are united together, so as never to be separated but by breaking them to pieces. One of those rattles singly, is incapable of producing sound, but the ringing of thirteen together, is sufficient to alarm the boldest man living.

"The Rattle-Snake is solitary, and associates with her kind only when it is necessary for their preservation. In winter, the warmth of a number together will preserve their lives, while singly, they would probably perish. The power of fascination attributed to her, by a generous construction, may be understood to mean, that those who consider the liberty and blessings which America affords, and once come over to her, never afterwards leave her, but spend their lives with her. She strongly resembles America in this, that she is beautiful in youth and her beauty increaseth with her age, 'her tongue also is blue and forked as the lightning, and her abode is among impenetrable rocks.'

—*An American Guesser*

"Like a man traveling in foggy weather, those at some distance before him on the road he sees wrapped up in the fog, as well as those behind him, and also the people in the fields on either side, but near him all appears clear, though in truth he is as much in the fog as any of them."

Franklin actually said to Thomas Jefferson, "Never contradict anybody."

Franklin wrote a letter to his daughter in January 1784, in which he questioned the propriety of using the bald eagle to symbolize America. In fact, the image of the eagle to be used was poorly drawn and looked more like a turkey. Franklin, somewhat tongue in cheek, extends his argument to the superiority of the turkey as a symbol for the United States. Amusingly enough, there are those in the American turkey processing industry who take Franklin seriously!

"For my own part I wish the Bald Eagle had not been chosen the Representative of our Country. He is a Bird of bad moral Character. He does not get his Living honestly. You may have seen him perched on some dead Tree near the River, where, too lazy to fish for himself, he watches the Labour of the Fishing Hawk; and when that diligent Bird has at length taken a Fish, and is bearing it to his Nest for the Support of his Mate and young Ones, the Bald Eagle pursues him and takes it from him.

"With all this Injustice, he is never in good Case but like those among Men who live by Sharping & Robbing he is generally poor and often very lousy. Besides he is a rank Coward: The little *King Bird* not bigger than a Sparrow attacks him boldly and drives him out of the District. He is therefore by no means a proper Emblem for the brave and honest Cincinnati of America who have driven all the *King birds* from our Country. . . .

"I am on this account not displeased that the Figure is not known as a Bald Eagle, but looks more like a Turkey. For the Truth the Turkey is in Comparison a much more respectable Bird, and withal a true original Native of America. . . . He is besides, though a little vain & silly, a Bird of Courage, and would not hesitate to attack a Grenadier of the British Guards who should presume to invade his Farm Yard with a red Coat on."

In the same letter, Franklin explains why he thought hereditary organizations were foolish:

"Honour worthily obtained (as for example that of our officers) is in its nature a personal thing and incommunicable to any but those who had some share in obtaining it. Thus among the Chinese, the most ancient and from long experience the wisest of nations, honour does not descend but ascends. [When a Chinese won it, the credit went to his parents.] This ascending honour is therefore useful to the state, as it encourages parents to give their children a good and virtuous education.

"But the descending honour, to posterity who could have no share in obtaining it, is not only groundless and absurd but often hurtful to that posterity, since it is apt to make them proud, disdaining to be employed in useful arts and thence falling into poverty and all the meannesses, servility, and wretchedness attending it; which is the present case with much of what is called the noblesse in Europe. . . .

"A man's son, for instance, is but half of his family, the other half belonging to the family of his wife. His son, too, marrying into another family, his share in the grandson is but a fourth. . . . In nine generations, which would not require more than three hundred years (no very great antiquity for a family), our present Chevalier of the Order of Cincinnatus's share in the then existing knight will be but a 512th part."

"[Do not] hold your head so high; stoop . . . stoop as you go through the world, and you'll miss many hard thumps."

"The Declaration of Independence only guarantees the American people the right to pursue happiness. You have to catch it yourself!"

"My parents had given me betimes religions impressions, and I received from my infancy a pious education in the principles of Calvinism. But scarcely was I arrived at fifteen years of age, when, after having doubted in turn of different tenets, according as I found them combated in the different books that I read, I began to doubt of Revelation itself. The time which I devoted to these exercises, and to reading, was the evening after my day's labor was finished, the morning before it began, and Sundays when I could escape divine service. While I lived with my father, he had insisted on my punctual attendance on public worship, and I still indeed considered it as a duty, but a duty which I thought I had no time to practice."

In Philadelphia, Franklin became associated with a printer named Keimer. Franklin wrote this about Keimer:

"He formed so high an opinion of my talents for refutation that he seriously proposed to me to become his colleague in the establishment of a new religious sect. He was to propagate the doctrine by preaching, and I to refute every opponent.

"When he explained to me his tenets, I found many absurdities which I refused to admit. . . . Keimer wore his beard long, because Moses had somewhere said, 'Thou shalt not mar the corners of thy beard.' He likewise observed the Sabbath; and these were with him two very essential points. I disliked them both."

At a later period, referring to his religious belief, Franklin wrote:

"Some volumes against Deism fell into my hands. They were said to be the substance of sermons preached at Boyle's Lecture. It happened that they produced on me an effect precisely the reverse of what was intended by the writers; for the arguments of the Deists, which were cited in order to be refuted, appealed to me much more forcibly than the refutation itself. In a word, I soon became a thorough Deist."

"I conceive, then, that the Infinite has created many beings or gods vastly superior to man."

"It may be these created gods are immortals; or it may be that after many ages, they are changed, and others supply their places."

"Howbeit, I conceive that each of these is exceeding good and very powerful; and that each has made for himself one glorious sun, attended with a beautiful and admirable system of planets."

"It is that particular wise and good God, who is the author and owner of our system, that I propose for the object of my praise and adoration."

"The faith you mention has doubtless its use in the world. I do not desire to see it diminished, nor would I desire to lessen it in any way; but I wish it were more productive of good works than I have generally seen it. I mean real good works, works of kindness, charity, mercy, and public spirit, not holy-day keeping, sermon-hearing, and reading, performing church ceremonies, or making long prayers, filled with flatteries and compliments, despised even by wise men, and much less capable of pleasing the Deity."

"It is pity that good works, among some sorts of people, are so little valued, and good words admired in their stead. I mean seemingly pious discourses, instead of humane, benevolent actions. These they almost put out of countenance by calling morality, rotten morality; righteousness, ragged righteousness, and even filthy rags, and when you mention virtue, pucker up their noses; at the same time that they eagerly snuff up an empty, canting harangue, as if it were a posy of the choicest flowers."

"Improvement in religion is called building up and edification. Faith is then the ground floor, hope is up one pair of stairs. . . . Don't delight so much to dwell in those lower rooms, but get as fast as you can into the garret; for in truth the best room in the house is charity. For my part I wish the house was turned upside down."

"By heaven, we understand a state of happiness, infinite in degree and eternal in duration. I can do nothing to deserve such a reward. He that, for giving a draught of water to a thirsty person, should expect to be paid with a good plantation, would be modest in his demands compared with those who think they deserve heaven for the little good they do on earth. . . . For my part, I have not the vanity to think I deserve it, the folly to expect, or the ambition to desire it."

"With regard to future bliss, I cannot help imagining that multitudes of the zealously orthodox of different sects, who at the last day may flock together in hopes of seeing each other damned, will be disappointed, and obliged to rest content with their own salvation."

"When religious people quarrel about religion, or hungry people about their victuals, it looks as if they had not much of either about them."

"A Swedish minister having assembled the chiefs of the Susquehanna Indians, made a sermon to them, acquainting them with the principal historical facts on which our religion is founded, such as the fall of our first parents by eating an apple; the coming of Christ to repair the mischief; his miracles and sufferings, etc.

."When he had finished, an Indian orator stood up to thank him. 'What you have told us,' said he, 'is all very good. It is indeed bad to eat apples. It is better to make them all into cider. We are much obliged by your kindness in coming so far to tell us those things which you have heard from your mothers. In return, I will tell you some of those which we have heard from ours. In the beginning, our fathers had only the flesh of animals to subsist on; and if their hunting was unsuccessful, they were starving. Two of our young hunters having killed deer, made a fire in the woods to broil some parts of it. When they were about to satisfy their hunger, they beheld a beautiful young woman descend from the clouds, and seat herself on that hill which you see yonder among the blue mountains. They said to each other, it is a spirit that perhaps has smelt our broiled venison and wishes to eat of it; let us offer some to her. They presented her with the tongue; she was pleased with the taste of it, and said, "Your kindness shall be rewarded. Come to this place after thirteen moons, and you shall find something that will be of a great benefit in nourishing you and your children to the latest generations." They did so and, to their surprise, found plants they had never seen before; but which, from that ancient time, have been constantly cultivated among us to our great advantage. Where her right hand touched the ground they found maize; where her left hand touched it they found kidney beans."

"The good missionary, disgusted with this idle tale, said, 'What I delivered to you were sacred truths; but what you tell me is mere fable, fiction, and falsehood."

"The Indian, offended, replied, 'My brother, it seems your friends have not done you justice in your education; they have not well instructed you in the rules of common civility. You saw that we, who understand and practice these rules, believed all your stories, why do you refuse to believe ours?' "

"Nowadays we have scarcely a little parson that does not think it the duty of every man within his reach to sit under his petty ministration, and that whoever omits this offends God. To such I wish more humility."

"A new town in the state of Massachusetts having done me the honor of naming itself after me, and proposing to build a steeple to their meeting house if I would give them a bell, I have advised the sparing themselves the expense of a steeple, for the present, and that they would accept of books instead of a bell, sense being preferred to sound."

When asked why he did not promulgate his rational views on religion, Franklin replied:

"The things of this world take up too much of my time, of which indeed I have too little left, to undertake anything like a reformation in religion."

At the age of eighty-four, just prior to his death, in reply to inquiries concerning his religious belief from Ezra Stiles, the president of Yale College, Franklin wrote:

"Here is my creed: I believe in one God, the Creator of the universe. That he governs it by his providence. That he ought to be worshiped. That the most acceptable service we render him is doing good to his other children. That the soul of man is immortal, and will be treated with justice in another life respecting its conduct in this."

Franklin's beloved *Poor Richard's Almanack* started in 1733 as a weather forecaster and a witty collection of homilies. Franklin wrote under the pseudonym of Richard Saunders, and the *Almanack* eventually became an annual that was published until 1757, selling as many as 10,000 issues a year. Franklin's two "big themes" emerged as frugality and the virtue of good work, but the maxims are remarkably wide-ranging in focus, and a surprising number are "household slogans" even to this day.

"A countryman between two lawyers is like a fish between two cats."

"A little neglect may breed mischief . . . for want of a nail, the shoe was lost; for want of a shoe the horse was lost; and for want of a horse the rider was lost."

"A man may, if he knows not how to save as he gets, keep his nose to the grindstone."

"A penny saved is a penny earned."

"Any fool can criticize, condemn and complain and most fools do."

"At twenty years of age, the will reigns; at thirty, the wit; and at forty, the judgment."

"Diligence is the Mother of good luck."

"Dost thou love life? Then do not squander time, for that's the stuff life is made of."

"Early morning hath gold in its mouth."

"Early to bed, early to rise makes a man healthy, wealthy, and wise."

"Energy and persistence conquer all things."

"Experience keeps a dear school, but fools will learn in no other."

"Genius without education is like silver in the mine."

"God helps them that help themselves."

"Haste makes waste."

"Having been poor is no shame, but being ashamed of it, is."

"He that blows the coals in quarrels that he has nothing to do with, has no right to complain if the sparks fly in his face."

"He that goes a-borrowing goes a-sorrowing."

"He that lives upon hope will die fasting."

"He who multiplies riches multiplies cares."

"Hide not your talents. They for use were made. What's a sundial in the shade?"

"If Jack's in love, he's no judge of Jill's beauty."

"If you would persuade, you must appeal to interest rather than intellect."

"It is hard for an empty bag to stand upright."

"Kill no more pigeons than you can eat."

"Little strokes fell great oaks."

"Many have been ruined by buying good pennyworths."

"Necessity never made a good bargain."

"Never confuse motion with action."

"Never leave that till to-morrow which you can do to-day."

"Plough deep while sluggards sleep, and you shall have corn to sell and to keep."

"Read much, but not many books."

"Some are weather-wise, some are otherwise."

"The sleeping fox catches no poultry."

"They that will not be counseled, cannot be helped. If you do not hear reason she will rap you on the knuckles."

"There is no kind of dishonesty into which otherwise good people more easily and frequently fall than that of defrauding the government."

"Think of these things, whence you came, where you are going, and to whom you must account."

"Three may keep a secret, if two of them are dead."

"Three removes are as bad as a fire."

"To find out a girl's faults, praise her to her girl friends."

"To lengthen thy Life, lessen thy meals."

"Vessels large may venture more, But little boats should keep near shore."

"Well done is better than well said."

"Whatever is begun in anger ends in shame."

"Where sense is wanting, everything is wanting."

"Wise men don't need advice. Fools won't take it."

"The world is full of fools and faint hearts; and yet everyone has courage enough to bear the misfortunes, and wisdom enough to manage the affairs, of his neighbor."

"Beware of little expenses. A small leak will sink a big ship."

"Blessed is he who expects nothing, for he will never be disappointed."

"Wealth is not his who has it but his who enjoys it."

"Creditors have better memories than debtors."

"He was so learned that he could name a horse in nine languages; so ignorant that he bought a cow to ride on."

"If a man could have half his wishes he could double his troubles."

"Guests, like fish, begin to smell after three days."

"Who is wise? He that learns from everyone. Who is powerful? He that governs his passions. Who is rich? He who is content. Who is that? Nobody."

"He that is of the opinion money will do everything may well be suspected of doing everything for money."

GEORGE WASHINGTON

(1732–1799)

First President of the United States

"Government is not reason, it is not eloquence, it is force; like fire, a troublesome servant and a fearfulsome master. Never for a moment should it be left to irresponsible action."

On the eve of his first inauguration: "My movements to the chair of government will

be accompanied by feelings not unlike
those of a culprit who is going to the place
of his execution."

"The United States of America should
have a foundation free from the influence
of clergy."

"It is impossible to rightly govern the
world without God and the Bible."

"Religious controversies are always productive of more acrimony and irreconcilable hatreds than those which spring from
any other cause."

"When we assumed the Soldier, we did
not lay aside the Citizen."

"Be courteous to all, but intimate with
few, and let those few be well tried before
you give them your confidence. True friendship is a plant of slow growth, and must
undergo and withstand the shocks of adversity before it is entitled to the appellation."

"Mankind, when left to themselves, are
unfit for their own government."

"Few men have virtue to withstand the
highest bidder."

"There can be no greater error than to expect, or calculate, upon real favors from nation to nation. It is an illusion which experience must cure, which a just pride ought to discard."

"I do not mean to exclude altogether the idea of patriotism. I know it exists, and I know it has done much in the present contest. But I will venture to assert, that a great and lasting war can never be supported on this principle alone. It must be aided by a prospect of interest, or some reward."

"To be prepared for war is one of the most effectual means of preserving peace."

"I hate deception, even where the imagination only is concerned."

"Liberty, when it begins to take root, is a plant of rapid growth."

"Men's opinions were as various as their faces."

From Washington's Military Farewell Address in November 1783:

"The singular interpositions of Providence in our feeble conditions were such as could scarcely escape the attention of the most observing."

Referring to himself in the third person:

"And being now to conclude these his [Washington's] last orders, to take his ultimate leave in a short time of the military character, and to bid a final adieu to the armies he has so long had the honor to command, he can only again offer in their behalf his recommendations to their grateful country, and his prayers to the God of armies. May ample justice be done them here, and may the choicest of Heaven's favors, both here and hereafter, attend those who, under Divine auspices, have secured innumerable blessings for others. With these wishes and this benediction, the Commander-in-chief is about to retire from service. The curtain of separation will soon be drawn, and the military scene to him will be closed forever."

ॐ

"As mankind becomes more liberal, they will be more apt to allow that all those who conduct themselves as worthy members of the community are equally entitled to the protections of civil government. I

hope ever to see America among the fore-
most nations of justice and liberality."

After his election, Washington was con-
tinually pursued by eager portrait painters.
"In for a penny, in for a pound, is an old
adage. I am so hackneyed to the touches of
the painters' pencils, that I am now altogether at their beck; and sit 'like Patience
on a monument' whilst they are delineating
the lines of my face. It is a proof, among
many others, of what habit and custom can
accomplish. At first I was as impatient and
as restive under the operation as a colt is of
the saddle. The next time I submitted very
reluctantly but with less flouncing. Now no
dray horse moves more rapidly to his thill
[one of the two shafts of a carriage or
wagon] than I do to the painter's chair."

"The successful termination of the war
has verified the most sanguine expecta-
tions; and my gratitude for the interposition
of Providence, and the assistance I have
received from my countrymen, increases
with every review of the momentous contest."

"I consider it an indispensable duty to
close this last solemn act of my official life,

by commending the interest of our dearest country to the protection of Almighty God, and those who have the superintendence of them to His holy keeping."

"I never mean, unless some particular circumstances should compel it, to possess another slave by purchase, it being among my first wishes to see some plan adopted, by which slavery in this country may be abolished by law."

Here are excerpts from Washington's First Inaugural Address on April 30, 1789:

"Such being the impressions under which I have, to obedience to the public summons, repaired to the present station, it would be peculiarly improper to omit, in this first official act, my fervent supplications to that Almighty Being, who rules over the universe, who presides in the councils of nations, and whose providential aids can supply every human defect, that His benediction may consecrate to the liberties and happiness of the people of the United States a government instituted by themselves for these essential purposes and may enable every instrument employed in its administration to execute with success the functions allotted to His charge. In tendering this homage to the great Author of every public and private good, I assure myself that it expresses your sentiments not less than my own, not those of my fellow citizens at large, less than either. . . .

"No people can be bound to acknowledge and adore the invisible hand which conducts the affairs of men more than the people of the United States. Every step by which they have advanced to the character of an independent nation seems to have been distinguished by some token of providential agency. . . .

"These reflections, arising out of the present crisis, have forced themselves too strongly on my mind to be suppressed. You will join with me, I trust, in thinking that there are none, under the influence of which the proceedings of a new and free government can more auspiciously commence. . . .

"We ought to be no less persuaded that the propitious smiles of Heaven can never be expected on a nation that disregards the eternal rules of order and right, which

Heaven itself has ordained. Having thus imparted to you my sentiments, as they have been awakened by the occasion which brings us together, I shall take my present leave; but not without resorting once more to the benign Parent of the human race, in humble supplication that, since He has been pleased to favor the American people with opportunities for deliberating in perfect tranquility, and dispositions for deciding with unparalleled unanimity on a form of government for the security of their union and the advancement of their happiness, so His divine blessing may be equally conspicuous in the enlarged views, the temperate consultation, and the wise measures, on which the success of this government may depend."

Washington's words at his Proclamation of the First National Thanksgiving on October 3, 1789:

"Whereas, it is the duty of all nations to acknowledge the Providence of Almighty God, to obey his will, to be grateful for His benefits, and humbly to implore his protection and favor; and, whereas, both Houses of Congress have, by their joint committee, requested me to recommend to the people

of the United States a day of public thanksgiving and prayer, to be observed by
acknowledging with grateful hearts the
many and signal favors of Almighty God,
especially by affording them an opportunity
peacably to establish a form of government
for their safety and happiness."

"Now, therefore, I do recommend and
assign Thursday, the twenty-sixth day of
November next, to be devoted by the people
of these States to the service of that great and
glorious Being, who is the beneficient Author
of all the good that was, that is, or that will
be; that we may then all unite in rendering
unto Him our sincere and humble thanks for
His kind care and protection of the people of
this country, previous to their becoming a
nation; for the signal and manifold mercies,
and the favorable interposition of His providence, in the course and conclusion of the
late war; for the great degree of tranquility,
union, and plenty, which we have since
enjoyed; for the peacable and rational manner in which we have been able to establish
constitutions of government for our safety
and happiness, and particularly the national
one now lately instituted; for the civil and
religious liberty with which we are blessed,
and the means we have of acquiring and

diffusing useful knowledge; and, in general, for all the great and various favors, which He has been pleased to confer upon us.

"And, also, that we may then unite in most humbly offering our prayers and supplications to the great Lord and Ruler of Nations, and beseech Him to pardon our national and other transgressions; to enable us all, whether in public or private stations, to perform our several and relative duties properly and punctually; to render our national government a blessing to all people, by constantly being a government of wise, just, and constitutional laws, discreetly and faithfully executed and obeyed; to protect and guide all sovereign and nations (especially such as have shown kindness to us), and to bless them with good governments, peace, and concord; to promote the knowledge and practice of true religion and virtue, and the increase of science, among them and us; and, generally, to grant unto all mankind such a degree of temporal prosperity as He alone knows to be best."

Washington's Proclamation for a Second National Thanksgiving on New Year's Day, 1795:

"When we review the calamities which afflict so many other nations, the present condition of the United States affords much manner of consolation and satisfaction. Our exemption hitherto from foreign war, and increasing prospect of the continuance of that exemption, the great degree of internal tranquility we have enjoyed, the recent confirmation of that tranquility by the suppression of an insurrection [the Whiskey Rebellion of 1794], which so wantonly threatened it, the happy course of our public affairs in general, the unexampled prosperity of all classes of our citizens, are circumstances which peculiarly mark our situation with indications of the Divine Beneficence towards us. In such a state of things it is in an especial manner our duty as a people, with devout reverence and affectionate gratitude, to acknowledge our many and great obligations to Almighty God, and to implore Him to continue and confirm the blessings we experience.

"Deeply penetrated with this sentiment, I, George Washington, President of the United States, do recommend to all religious societies and denominations, and to all persons whomsoever within the United States, to set apart and observe Thursday,

the 19th day of February next, as a day of
public thanksgiving and prayer, and on that
day to meet together and render their sincere and hearty thanks to the Great ruler of
nations for the manifold and signal mercies
which distinguish our lot as a nation; particularly for the possession of constitutions
of government, which unite, and by their
union establish, liberty and order; for the
preservation of our peace, foreign and
domestic; for the seasonable control which
has been given to a spirit of disorder in the
suppression of the late insurrection; and,
generally, for the prosperous course of our
affairs public and private; and at the same
time humbly and fervently to beseech the
kind Author of those blessings graciously to
prolong them to us; to imprint on our
hearts a deep and solemn sense of our obligations to Him for them; to teach us rightly
to estimate their immense value; to preserve us from the arrogance of prosperity,
and from hazarding the advantages we
enjoy by the delusive pursuits;to dispose us
to merit the continuance of His favors by
not abusing them, by our gratitude for
them, and by a correspondent conduct as
citizens and as men; to render this country
more and more a safe and propitious asy-
lum for the unfortunate of other countries;

to extend among us true and useful knowledge; to diffuse and establish habits of
sobriety, order, morality, and piety; and
finally to impart all the blessings we possess, or ask for ourselves, to the whole family of mankind.

"In testimony whereof, I have caused
the seal of the United States of America to
be affixed to these presents, and signed the
same with my hand. Done at the city of
Philadelphia, this first day of January, one
thousand seven hundred and ninety-five
and of the independence of the United
States of America the nineteenth."

From Washington's Farewell Address,
September 17, 1796:

"Of all the dispositions and habits which
lead to political prosperity, Religion and
Morality are indispensable supports. In vain
would that man claim the tribute of
Patriotism, who should labor to subvert
these great pillars of human happiness,
these firmest props of the duties of Men
and Citizens. The mere Politician, equally
with the pious man, ought to respect and
cherish them. A volume could not trace all
their connections with private and public

felicity. Let it simply be asked, Where is the security for property, for reputation, for life, if the sense of religious obligation *desert* the oaths which are the instruments of investigation in Courts of Justice? And let us with caution indulge the supposition that morality can be maintained without religion. Whatever may be conceded to the influence of refined education on minds of peculiar structure, reason and experience both forbid us to expect that national morality can prevail in exclusion of religious principle.

"It is substantially true that virtue or morality is a necessary spring of popular government. The rule, indeed, extends with more of less force to every species of free government. Who, that is a sincere friend to it, can look with indifference upon attempts to shake the foundation of the fabric? . . .

"Observe good faith and justice towards all Nations; cultivate peace and harmony with all. Religion and Morality enjoin this conduct; and can it be that good policy does not equally enjoin it? It will be worthy of a free, enlightened, and, at no distant period, a great Nation, to give to mankind the mag-

nanimous and too novel example of a people always guided by an exalted justice and
benevolence. Who can doubt, that, in the
course of time and things, the fruits of such
a plan would richly repay any temporary
advantages, which might be lost by a steady
adherence to it? Can it be that Providence
has not connected the permanent felicity of
a nation with its Virtue? The experiment, at
least, is recommended by every sentiment
which ennobles human nature."

JOHN ADAMS

(1735–1826)

Second President of the United States

"The government of the United States is not, in any sense, founded on the Christian religion."

"Let the human mind loose. It must be loose. It will be loose. Superstition and dogmatism cannot confine it."

"Love sweetens life."

"Virtue is not always amiable."

"A pen is certainly an excellent instrument to fix a man's attention and to inflame his ambition."

"Remember, democracy never lasts long. It soon wastes, exhausts, and murders itself. There never was a democracy yet that did not commit suicide."

"A government of laws, and not of men."

"Facts are stubborn things; and whatever may be our wishes, our inclinations, or the dictates of our passions, they cannot alter the state of facts and evidence."

"I agree with you that in politics the middle way is none at all."

"The Revolution was effected before the War commenced. The Revolution was in the minds and hearts of the people; a change in their religious sentiments of their duties and obligations. . . . This radical change in the principles, opinions, sentiments, and affections of the people, was the real American Revolution."

"I must study politics and war that my sons may have liberty to study mathematics and philosophy."

"I always consider the settlement of America with reverence and wonder, as the opening of a grand scene and design in providence, for the illumination of the ignorant and the emancipation of the slavish part of mankind all over the earth."

"The happiness of society is the end of government."

"There is danger from all men. The only maxim of a free government ought to be to trust no man living with power to endanger the public liberty."

"Fear is the foundation of most governments."

"Inequality of Mind and Body are so established by God Almighty in his Constitution of Human Nature that no art or policy can ever plane them down to a level."

"The essence of a free government consists in an effectual control of rivalries."

"It is weakness rather than wickedness which renders men unfit to be trusted with unlimited power."

"I was of an amorous disposition and very early from ten or eleven Years of Age, was very fond of the Society of Females."

On his tenure as vice president: "My country has in its wisdom contrived for me the most insignificant office that ever the invention of man contrived or his imagination conceived."

Writing to his wife, Abigail, on his second evening in the damp, unfurnished White House:

"Before I end my letter, I pray Heaven to bestow the best of Blessings on this House and all that shall hereafter inhabit it. May none but honest and wise Men ever rule under this roof."

"Happy [George] Washington! Happy to be childless! My children give me more pain than all my Enemies."

"As I understand the Christian religion, it was, and is, a revelation. But how has it happened that millions of fables, tales, legends, have been blended with both Jewish and Christian revelation that have made them the most bloody religion that ever existed."

"I never write or talk upon divinity. I have had more than I could do of humanity."

"Remember the Index Expurgatorius, the inquisition, the stake, the axe, the halter, and the guillotine; and, oh! horrible, the rack!"

"A bank that issues paper interest is a pickpocket or a robber."

Adams loathed Alexander Hamilton:

"[Hamilton], like the worm at the root of the peach, did labor for twelve years, underground and in darkness, to girdle the root, while all the axes of the anti-Federalists, Democrats, Jacobins, Virginia debtors to English merchants, and French hirelings, chopping as they were for the whole time at the trunk, could not fell the tree."

No humble New Englander was Adams:

"Boston Town Meetings and our Harvard College have set the universe in motion."

"Ennui, when it rains on a man in large drops, is worse than one of our northeast storms; but the labors of agriculture and amusement of letters will shelter me."

"Have you considered that system of holy lies and pious frauds that has raged and triumphed for 1500 years."

Adams wrote this unflattering verse about his fellow attorneys:

"You ask me why Lawyers so much are increased
Tho much of the Country already are fleeced
The Reason I'm sure is most strikingly plain
The Sheep are oft sheared yet the Wool grows again."

Adams urged his son John Quincy to get out of politics, even if it meant "you should be obliged to live on turnips, potatoes, and cabbage, as I am. My sphere is reduced to my garden, and so must yours be."

Adams was certain that history would misremember him and his tenure during the American struggle for independence. That history, he predicted, "will be one continued lie from one end to the other. The essence of the whole will be that Dr. Franklin's electrical rod smote the earth and out sprang General Washington. That Franklin electrified him with his rod—and thenceforward these two conducted all the policy, negotiations, legislatures, and war."

"The question before the human race is, whether the God of nature shall govern the world by his own laws, or whether priests and kings shall rule it by fictitious miracles."

Adams was a lover of books: "You will never be alone with a poet in your pocket."

Adams maintained that he had discovered "that Men find Ways to persuade themselves to believe any Absurdity, to submit to any Prostitution, rather than forgo their Wishes and Desires. Their Reason becomes at last an eloquent Advocate on the Side of their Passions and [they] bring themselves to believe that black is white, that Vice is Virtue, that Folly is Wisdom, and Eternity a Moment."

"Human nature cannot bear prosperity. It invariably intoxicates individuals and nations. Adversity is the great reformer. Affliction is the purifying furnace."

"If I were to go over my Life again, I would be a shoemaker rather than an American statesman."

"No man who ever held the office of president would congratulate a friend on obtaining it. You will make one man ungrateful, and a hundred men his enemies, for every office he can bestow."

After the death of his beloved 74-year-old wife Abigail in 1818, Adams told a friend, "My house is a Region of sorrow. Never in my whole life was I more perplexed or distressed than at this moment."

In the last month of his life, Adams told Noah Webster, "I inhabit a weak, frail, decayed tenement, open to the winds and broken in upon by the storms. What is worse, from all I can learn, the landlord does not intend to repair."

On July 4, 1826, Adams whispered his last words, concerning his old friend: "Thomas Jefferson survives." But in fact, Jefferson had died at Monticello just a few hours earlier.

THOMAS JEFFERSON

(1743–1826)

Third President of the United States

Surely no American has ever summoned more eloquence on the subject of "inalienable" human rights than Thomas Jefferson. Here are a number of his written and spoken remarks on the subject that was dearest to his heart.

From the Declaration of Independence, as originally written by Jefferson:

"We hold these truths to be self-evident, that all men are created equal; that they are endowed by their Creator with inherent and inalienable rights; that among these, are life, liberty, and the pursuit of happiness; that to secure these rights, governments are instituted among men, deriving their just powers from the consent of the governed; that whenever any form of government becomes destructive of these ends, it is the right of the people to alter or abolish it, and to institute new government, laying its foundation on such principles, and organizing its powers in such form, as to them shall seem most likely to effect their safety and happiness."

"[Our] principles [are] founded on the immovable basis of equal right and reason."

"An equal application of law to every condition of man is fundamental."

"The most sacred of the duties of a government [is] to do equal and impartial justice to all its citizens."

"To unequal privileges among members of the same society the spirit of our nation is, with one accord, adverse."

"In America, no other distinction between man and man had ever been known but that of persons in office exercising powers by authority of the laws, and private individuals. Among these last, the poorest laborer stood on equal ground with the wealthiest millionaire, and generally on a more favored one whenever their rights seem to jar."

"Of distinction by birth or badge, [Americans] had no more idea than they had of the mode of existence in the moon or planets. They had heard only that there were such, and knew that they must be wrong."

"[The] best principles [of our republic] secure to all its citizens a perfect equality of rights."

"The principles on which we engaged, of which the charter of our independence is the record, were sanctioned by the laws of our being, and we but obeyed them in pursuing undeviatingly the course they called for. It issued finally in that inestimable state of freedom which alone can ensure to man the enjoyment of his equal rights."

"Man [is] a rational animal, endowed by nature with rights and with an innate sense of justice."

"A free people [claim] their rights as derived from the laws of nature, and not as the gift of their chief magistrate."

"Under the law of nature, all men are born free, every one comes into the world with a right to his own person, which includes the liberty of moving and using it at his own will. This is what is called personal liberty, and is given him by the Author of nature, because necessary for his own sustenance."

"What is true of every member of the society, individually, is true of them all collectively; since the rights of the whole can be no more than the sum of the rights of the individuals."

"The evidence of [the] natural right [of expatriation], like that of our right to life, liberty, the use of our faculties, the pursuit of happiness, is not left to the feeble and sophistical investigations of reason, but is impressed on the sense of every man. We do not claim these under the charters of kings or legislators, but under the King of Kings."

"Natural rights [are] the objects for the protection of which society is formed and municipal laws established."

"Can the liberties of a nation be thought secure when we have removed their only firm basis, a conviction in the minds of the people that these liberties are of the gift of God? That they are not to be violated but with His wrath."

"Questions of natural right are triable by their conformity with the moral sense and reason of man."

"It is a principle that the right to a thing gives a right to the means without which it could not be used, that is to say, that the means follow their end."

"The right to use a thing comprehends a right to the means necessary to its use, and without which it would be useless."

"The Declaration of Independence . . .
[is the] declaratory charter of our rights,
and of the rights of man."

"Some other natural rights . . . [have]
not yet entered into any declaration of
rights."

"I shall see with sincere satisfaction the
progress of those sentiments which tend to
restore to man all his natural rights, convinced he has no natural right in opposition
to his social duties."

"The God who gave us life gave us liberty at the same time; the hand of force
may destroy, but cannot disjoin them."

"Of liberty I would say that, in the whole
plenitude of its extent, it is unobstructed
action according to our will. But rightful
liberty is unobstructed action according to
our will within limits drawn around us by
the equal rights of others. I do not add
'within the limits of the law,' because law is
often but the tyrant's will, and always so
when it violates the right of an individual."

"That liberty [is pure] which is to go to
all, and not to the few or the rich alone."

"In a government bottomed on the will of all, the life and liberty of every individual citizen becomes interesting to all."

"I would rather be exposed to the inconveniences [of those] attending too much liberty than to those attending too small a degree of it."

"Being myself a warm zealot for the attainment and enjoyment by all mankind of as much liberty as each may exercise without injury to the equal liberty of his fellow citizens, I have lamented that . . . the endeavors to obtain this should have been attended with the effusion of so much blood."

On "The Pursuit of Happiness," Jefferson was no less eloquent:

"The Giver of life gave it for happiness and not for wretchedness."

"If [God] has made it a law in the nature of man to pursue his own happiness, He has left him free in the choice of place as well as mode, and we may safely call on the whole body of English jurists to produce the map on which nature has traced

for each individual the geographical line
which she forbids him to cross in pursuit of
happiness."

"Perfect happiness, I believe, was never
intended by the Deity to be the lot of one of
his creatures in this world; but that he has
very much put in our power the nearness
of our approaches to it, is what I as stead-
fastly believe."

"The freedom and happiness of man . . .
[are] the sole objects of all legitimate government."

"[It is a] great truth that industry, commerce and security are the surest roads
to the happiness and prosperity of [a]
people."

"The only orthodox object of the institution of government is to secure the greatest
degree of happiness possible to the general
mass of those associated under it."

"I sincerely pray that all the members of
the human family may, in the time prescribed by the Father of us all, find themselves securely established in the enjoyment of life, liberty, and happiness."

‿

"To secure these [inalienable] rights [to
life, liberty, and the pursuit of happiness],
governments are instituted among men,
deriving their just powers from the consent
of the governed. . . . Whenever any form of
government becomes destructive of these
ends, it is the right of the people to alter or
abolish it, and to institute new government,
laying its foundation on such principles,
and organizing its powers in such form, as
to them shall seem most likely to effect
their safety and happiness."

"The principles of government . . . [are]
founded in the rights of man."

"It is to secure our rights that we resort
to government at all."

"The idea is quite unfounded that on
entering into society we give up any natural
right."

"[These are] the rights which God and
the laws have given equally and independ-
ently to all."

"For the ordinary safety of the citizens
of the several States, whether against

dangers from within or without, reliance
has been placed either on the domestic
means of the individuals or on those provided by the respective States."

"[It is the obligation] of every government to yield protection to their citizens as
the consideration for their obedience."

Here's Jefferson on the nature of the
actual endeavor to secure rights:

"The spirit of the times may alter, will
alter. Our rulers will become corrupt, our
people careless. A single zealot may commence [as] persecutor, and better men be
his victims. It can never be too often
repeated that the time for fixing every
essential right on a legal basis is while
our rulers are honest and ourselves
united. From the conclusion of [their] war
[for independence, a nation begins] going
down hill. It will not then be necessary to
resort every moment to the people for
support. They will be forgotten, therefore,
and their rights disregarded. They will
forget themselves but in the sole faculty
of making money, and will never think of
uniting to effect a due respect for their
rights. The shackles, therefore, which

shall not be knocked off at the conclusion of [that] war will remain on [them] long, will be made heavier and heavier, till [their] rights shall revive or expire in a convulsion."

"What a cruel reflection that a rich country cannot long be a free one."

"[If] a positive declaration of some essential rights could not be obtained in the requisite latitude, [the] answer [is], Half a loaf is better than no bread. If we cannot secure all our rights, let us secure what we can."

"Circumstances sometimes require, that rights the most unquestionable should be advanced with delicacy."

"In endeavors to improve our situation, we should never despair."

"The ground of liberty is to be gained by inches, [and] we must be contented to secure what we can get from time to time and eternally press forward for what is yet to get. It takes time to persuade men to do even what is for their own good."

"Instead of that liberty which takes root and growth in the progress of reason, if recovered by mere force or accident, it becomes with an unprepared people a tyranny still of the many, the few, or the one."

On restrictions on natural rights, Jefferson was cautious and pensive:

"All . . . natural rights may be abridged or regulated in [their] exercise by law."

"Our rulers can have authority over such natural rights only as we have submitted to them."

"Every man, and every body of men on earth, possesses the right of self-government. . . . This, like all other natural rights, may be abridged or modified in its exercise by their own consent, or by the law of those who depute them, if they meet in the right of others."

"Were [a right] to be refused, or to be so shackled by regulations, not necessary for . . . peace and safety . . . as to render its use impracticable . . . it would then be an injury, of which we should be entitled to demand redress."

"Measures against right should be mollified in their exercise, if it be wished to lengthen them to the greatest term possible."

"I had hoped that [nations were] familiarized to such a degree of liberty, that they might without difficulty or danger fill up the measure to its *maximum*; a term which, though in the insulated man, bounded only by his natural powers, must in society be so far restricted as to protect himself against the evil passions of his associates and consequently, them against him."

"Laws abridging the natural right of the citizen should be restrained by rigorous constructions within their narrowest limits."

"It had become an universal and almost uncontroverted position in the several States, that the purposes of society do not require a surrender of all our rights to our ordinary governors; that there are certain portions of right not necessary to enable them to carry on an effective government, and which experience has nevertheless proved they will be constantly encroaching on, if submitted to them; that there are also certain fences which

experience has proved peculiarly efficacious against wrong, and rarely obstruc-
tive of right, which yet the governing
powers have ever shown a disposition to
weaken and remove. Of the first kind, for
instance, is freedom of religion; of the
second, trial by jury, habeas corpus laws,
free presses."

"If we are made in some degree for
others, yet in a greater [sense] are we
made for ourselves. It were contrary to
feeling and indeed ridiculous to suppose
that a man had less rights in himself than
one of his neighbors, or all of them put
together. This would be slavery, and not
that liberty which the bill of rights has
made inviolable, and for the preservation
of which our government has been
charged."

"No one has a right to obstruct another
exercising his faculties innocently for the
relief of sensibilities made a part of his
nature."

"No man has a natural right to commit
aggression on the equal rights of another,
and this is all from which the laws ought to
restrain him."

"We may consider each generation as a distinct nation, with a right, by the will of its majority, to bind themselves, but none to bind the succeeding generation, more than the inhabitants of another country."

"[As to] the question whether, by the laws of nature, one generation of men can, by any act of theirs, bind those which are to follow them? I say, by the laws of nature, there being between generation and generation, as between nation and nation, no other obligatory law."

"I may err in my measures, but never shall deflect from the intention to fortify the public liberty by every possible means, and to put it out of the power of the few to riot on the labors of the many."

"[Oppose] with manly firmness [any] invasions on the rights of the people."

Jefferson was the most articulate and reasonable early American when it came to explicating morality and moral principles—the conduct that is proper between and among citizens. He wrote volumes on the subject, and returned to it throughout his philosophical life. Here are some excerpts:

"God . . . has formed us moral agents
. . . that we may promote the happiness of
those with whom He has placed us in society, by acting honestly towards all, benevo-
lently to those who fall within our way,
respecting sacredly their rights, bodily and
mental, and cherishing especially their
freedom of conscience, as we value our
own."

"Peace, prosperity, liberty and morals
have an intimate connection."

On the true nature of virtue and happiness:

"Without virtue, happiness cannot be."

"The order of nature [is] that individual
happiness shall be inseparable from the
practice of virtue."

"Liberty . . . is the great parent of science and of virtue; and . . . a nation will be
great in both always in proportion as it is
free."

On the importance of honesty in any
moral system:

"Truth is certainly a branch of morality, and a very important one to society."

"Follow truth as the only safe guide, and . . . eschew error, which bewilders us in one false consequence after another."

"Truth being as cheap as error, it is as well to rectify [an error of fact] for our own satisfaction."

"Honesty is the first chapter in the book of wisdom."

"Honesty, disinterestedness and good nature are indispensable to procure the esteem and confidence of those with whom we live, and on whose esteem our happiness depends."

On what Jefferson delineated as "the moral sense" and "the moral instinct":

"I sincerely . . . believe . . . in the general existence of a moral instinct. I think it the brightest gem with which the human character is studded, and the want of it as more degrading than the most hideous of the bodily deformities."

"He who made us would have been a piti-
ful bungler, if he had made the rules of our
moral conduct a matter of science. For one
man of science, there are thousands who are
not. What would have become of them? Man
was destined for society. His morality, therefore, was to be formed to this object. He was
endowed with a sense of right and wrong
merely relative to this. This sense is as much
a part of his nature, as the sense of hearing,
seeing, feeling; it is the true foundation of
morality. . . . The moral sense, or conscience,
is as much a part of man as his leg or arm. It
is given to all human beings in a stronger or
weaker degree, as force of members is given
them in a greater or lesser degree. It may be
strengthened by exercise, as may any particular limb of the body. This sense is submitted
indeed in some degree to the guidance of
reason; but it is a small stock which is
required for this: even a less one than what
we call Common sense. State a moral case to
a ploughman and a professor. The former
will decide it as well, and often better than
the latter, because he has not been led astray
by artificial rules."

"How necessary was the care of the
Creator in making the moral principle so
much a part of our constitution as that no

errors of reasoning or of speculation might lead us astray from its observance in practice."

"Morals were too essential to the happiness of man, to be risked on the uncertain combinations of the head. [Nature] laid their foundation, therefore, in sentiment, not in science."

"I believe . . . that [justice] is instinct and innate, that the moral sense is as much a part of our constitution as that of feeling, seeing, or hearing; as a wise Creator must have seen to be necessary in an animal destined to live in society."

"The moral law of our nature . . . [is] the moral law to which man has been subjected by his Creator, and of which his feelings or conscience, as it is sometimes called, are the evidence with which his Creator has furnished him."

"Conscience [is] the only sure clue which will eternally guide a man clear of all doubts and inconsistencies."

"Experience proves that the moral and physical qualities of man, whether good or evil, are transmissible in a certain degree from father to son."

"[It is a] general truth that great men will think alike and act alike, though without intercommunication."

"The true fountains of evidence [are] the head and heart of every rational and honest man. It is there nature has written her moral laws, and where every man may read them for himself."

"Assuming the fact that the earth has been created in time and consequently the dogma of final causes, we yield, of course, to this short syllogism: Man was created for social intercourse; but social intercourse cannot be maintained without a sense of justice; then man must have been created with a sense of justice."

"Egoism, in a broader sense, has been . . . presented as the source of moral action. It has been said that we feed the hungry, clothe the naked, bind up the wounds of the man beaten by thieves, pour oil and wine into them, set him on our own beast and bring him to the inn, because we receive ourselves pleasure from these acts.

. . . These good acts give us pleasure, but how happens it that they give us pleasure? Because nature hath implanted in our breasts a love of others, a sense of duty to them, a moral instinct, in short, which prompts us irresistibly to feel and to succor their distresses. . . . The Creator would indeed have been a bungling artist had he intended man for a social animal without planting in him social dispositions. It is true they are not planted in every man, because there is no rule without exceptions; but it is false reasoning which converts exceptions into the general rule."

"That a man owes no duty to which he is not urged by some impulsive feeling . . . is correct, if referred to the standard of general feeling in the given case, and not to the feeling of a single individual."

"Self-interest, or rather self-love, or *egoism,* has been more plausibly substituted as the basis of morality. But I consider our relations with others as constituting the boundaries of morality. With ourselves, we stand on the ground of identity, not of relation, which last, requiring two subjects, excludes self-love confined to a single one. To ourselves, in strict language, we can

owe no duties, obligation requiring also
two parties. Self-love, therefore, is no part
of morality. Indeed, it is exactly its counter-
part."

"I believe . . . that every human mind
feels pleasure in doing good to another."

"The practice of morality being necessary for the well-being of society, [our
Creator] has taken care to impress its precepts so indelibly on our hearts that they
shall not be effaced by the subtleties of our
brain."

"The want or imperfection of the moral
sense in some men, like the want or imperfection of the senses of sight and hearing in
others, is no proof that it is a general characteristic of the species."

"The non-existence of justice is not to be
inferred from the fact that the same act is
deemed virtuous and right in one society
which is held vicious and wrong in another;
because as the circumstances and opinions
of different societies vary, so the acts which
may do them right or wrong must vary also;
for virtue does not consist in the act we do,
but in the end it is to effect."

"Circumstances must always yield to substance."

"If [an act] is to effect the happiness of him to whom it is directed, it is virtuous; while in a society under different circumstances and opinions the same act might produce pain and would be vicious. The essence of virtue is in doing good to others, while what is good may be one thing in one society and its contrary in another."

"Our part is to pursue with steadiness what is right, turning neither to right nor left for the intrigues or popular delusions of the day, assured that the public approbation will in the end be with us."

"A conviction that we are right accomplishes half the difficulty of correcting wrong."

"Everyone is bound to bear witness, where wrong has been done."

"The laws of [our] country . . . in offenses within their cognizance, compel those who have knowledge of a fact to declare it for the purposes of justice and of the general good and safety of society. And certainly, where wrong has been done, he who knows and conceals the doer of it makes himself an accomplice, and justly censurable as such."

"Perseverance in object, though not by the most direct way, is often more laudable than perpetual changes, as often as the object shifts light."

"A bold, unequivocal virtue is the best handmaid even to ambition, and would carry [one] further, in the end, than [the pursuit of a] temporizing, wavering policy."

"Men are disposed to live honestly, if the means of doing so are open to them."

"Unequivocal in principle, reasonable in manner, we shall be able I hope to do a great deal of good to the cause of freedom and harmony."

"I have ever deemed it more honorable and more profitable, too, to set a good example than to follow a bad one."

"The only exact testimony of a man is his actions, leaving the reader to pronounce on them his own judgment."

"The entertainments of fiction are useful as well as pleasant. . . . Everything is useful which contributes to fix us in the principles and practice of virtue. When any signal act of charity or of gratitude, for instance, is presented either to our sight or imagination, we are deeply impressed with its beauty and feel a strong desire in ourselves of doing charitable and grateful acts also. On the contrary, when we see or read of any atrocious deed, we are disgusted with its deformity and conceive an abhorrence of vice. Now every emotion of this kind is an exercise of our virtuous dispositions; and dispositions of the mind, like limbs of the body, acquire strength by exercise. But exercise produces habit, and in the instance of which we speak, the exercise being of the moral feelings, produces a habit of thinking and acting virtuously."

"Considering history as a moral exercise, her lessons would be too infrequent if confined to real life. Of those recorded by historians few incidents have been attended with such circumstances as to excite in any high degree this sympathetic emotion of virtue. We are, therefore, wisely framed to be as warmly interested for a fictitious as for a real personage. The spacious field of imagination is thus laid open to our use, and lessons may be formed to illustrate and carry home to the heart every moral rule of life. Thus a lively and lasting sense of filial duty is more effectually impressed on the mind of a son or daughter by reading *King Lear*, than by all the dry volumes of ethics and divinity that ever were written."

"History, in general, only informs us what bad government is."

"The sentiments of men are known not only by what they receive, but what they reject also."

"Most virtues when carried beyond certain bounds degenerate into vices."

"It is reasonable that every one who asks justice should do justice."

"The art of life is the art of avoiding pain; and he is the best pilot, who steers clearest of the rocks and shoals with which it is beset."

"A nation, as a society, forms a moral person, and every member of it is personally responsible for his society."

"Moral duties [are] as obligatory on nations as on individuals."

"The laws of humanity make it a duty for nations, as well as individuals, to succor those whom accident and distress have thrown upon them."

"The moral duties which exist between individual and individual in a state of nature accompany them into a state of society, and the aggregate of the duties of all the individuals composing the society constitutes the duties of that society towards any other; so that between society and society the same moral duties exist as did between the individuals composing them while in an unassociated state, and their Maker not having released them from those duties on their forming themselves into a nation. Compacts, then, between nation and nation are obligatory on them by the same moral law which obliges individuals to observe their compacts."

"We are firmly convinced, and we act on that conviction, that with nations as with individuals, our interests soundly calculated will ever be found inseparable from our moral duties."

"Political interest [can] never be separated in the long run from moral right."

"Honesty and interest are as intimately connected in the public as in the private code of morality."

"So invariably do the laws of nature create our duties and interests, that when they seem to be at variance, we ought to suspect some fallacy in our reasonings."

"Good faith . . . ought ever to be the rule of action in public as well as in private transactions."

"I never did, or countenanced, in public life, a single act inconsistent with the strictest good faith; having never believed there was one code of morality for a public, and another for a private man."

"It is strangely absurd to suppose that a million of human beings, collected together, are not under the same moral laws which bind each of them separately."

"If the morality of one man produces a just line of conduct in him acting individually, why should not the morality of one hundred men produce a just line of conduct in them acting together?"

"What is true of every member of the society, individually, is true of them all collectively; since the rights of the whole can be no more than the sum of the rights of the individuals."

Finally, Jefferson addressed with consummate clarity the issues surrounding morality in government and its administration:

"When we come to the moral principles on which the government is to be administered, we come to what is proper for all conditions of society. . . . Liberty, truth, probity, honor, are declared to be the four cardinal principles of society. I believe . . . that morality, compassion, generosity, are innate elements of the human constitution; that there exists a right independent of force."

"[I consider] ethics, as well as religion, as supplements to law in the government of man."

"Is it the less dishonest to do what is wrong, because not expressly prohibited by written law? Let us hope our moral principles are not yet in that stage of degeneracy."

To George Washington: "Our countrymen are in the precious habit of considering right as a barrier against all solicitation."

"It is rare that the public sentiment decides immorally or unwisely, and the individual who differs from it ought to distrust and examine well his own opinion."

"That every man shall be made virtuous by any process whatever is, indeed, no more to be expected than that every tree shall be made to bear fruit, and every plant nourishment. The brier and bramble can never become the vine and olive; but their asperities may be softened by culture, and their properties improved to usefulness in the order and economy of the world."

"I know but one code of morality for man whether acting singly or collectively. He who says I will be a rogue when I act in company with a hundred others, but an honest man when I act alone, will be believed in the former assertion, but not in the latter."

Jefferson warned of the dangers of selfishness ("self-love"), and offered prescription or two for counteracting it:

"Self-love . . . is the sole antagonist of virtue, leading us constantly by our propensities to self-gratification in violation of our moral duties to others. Accordingly, it is against this enemy that are erected the batteries of moralists and religionists, as the only obstacle to the practice of morality. Take from man his selfish propensities, and he can have nothing to seduce him from the practice of virtue. Or subdue those propensities by education, instruction, or restraint, and virtue remains without a competitor."

"A regard for reputation and the judgment of the world may sometimes be felt where conscience is dormant."

"I fear, from the experience of the last twenty-five years, that morals do not of necessity advance hand in hand with the sciences."

Jefferson worried that the United States would abandon morality along its way:

"In every government on earth is some trace of human weakness, some germ of corruption and degeneracy, which cunning will discover, and wickedness insensibly open, cultivate and improve."

"What institution is insusceptible of abuse in wicked hands?"

"Mankind soon learn to make interested uses of every right and power which they possess, or may assume."

"The nation who [has] never admitted a chapter of morality into her political code . . . [will] boldly [avow] that whatever power [she] can make hers is hers of right."

"It was not expected in this age, that nations so honorably distinguished by their advances in science and civilization, would suddenly cast away the esteem they had merited from the world and, revolting from the empire of morality, assume a character in history which all the tears of their posterity will never wash from its pages."

"I do not believe with the Rochefoucaults and the Montaignes that fourteen out of fifteen men are rogues. I believe a great abatement from that proportion may be made in favor of general honesty. But I have always found that rogues would be uppermost, and I do not know that the proportion is too strong for the higher orders and for those who, rising above the swinish multitude, always contrive to nestle themselves into the places of power and profit. These rogues set out with stealing the people's good opinion, and then steal from them the right of withdrawing it, by contriving laws and associations against the power of the people themselves."

"Such is the moral construction of the world, that no national crime passes unpunished in the long run. . . . Were your present oppressors to reflect on the same truth, they would spare to their own countries the penalties on their present wrongs which will be inflicted on them in future times. The seeds of hatred and revenge which they [sow] with a large hand will not fail to produce their fruits in time. Like their brother robbers on the highway, they suppose the escape of the moment a final escape and deem infamy and future risk countervailed by present gain."

"Crooked schemes will end by overwhelming their authors and coadjutors in disgrace, and . . . he alone who walks strict and upright, and who, in matters of opinion, will be contented that others should be as free as himself, and acquiesce when his opinion is fairly overruled, will attain his object in the end."

"If pride of character be of worth at any time, it is when it disarms the efforts of malice."

"There are various ways of keeping truth out of sight."

"In truth, I do not recollect in all the animal kingdom a single species but man which is eternally and systematically engaged in the destruction of its own species. What is called civilization seems to have no other effect on him than to teach him to pursue the principle of *bellum omnium in omnia* [war of all against all] on a larger scale, and in place of the little contests of tribe against tribe, to engage all the quarters of the earth in the same work of destruction. When we add to this that as to the other species of animals, the lions and tigers are mere lambs compared with man as a destroyer, we must conclude that it is in man alone that nature has been able to find a sufficient barrier against the too great multiplication of other animals and of man himself, an equilibrating power against the fecundity of generation."

"When great evils happen, I am in the habit of looking out for what good may arise from them as consolations to us, and Providence has in fact so established the order of things, as that most evils are the means of producing some good."

On the evils of force and corruption:

"I have never been able to conceive how any rational being could propose happiness to himself from the exercise of power over others."

"Force [is] the vital principle and immediate parent of despotism."

"Either force or corruption has been the principle of every modern government."

"Force cannot change right."

"With the laborers of England generally, does not the moral coercion of want subject their will as despotically to that of their employer, as the physical constraint does the soldier, the seaman, or the slave?"

"[When] the principle that force is right becomes the principle of the nation itself, they would not permit an honest minister, were accident to bring such an one into power, to relax their system of lawless piracy."

Though he was himself a wealthy man, Jefferson was not impervious to the various corruptions that wealth can bring about:

"My observations do not enable me to say I think integrity the characteristic of wealth. In general, I believe the decisions of the people in a body will be more honest and more disinterested than those of wealthy men, and I can never doubt an attachment to his country in any man who has his family and [private property] in it."

"I may further say that I have not observed men's honesty to increase with their riches."

"Wealth, title, office, are no recommendations to my friendship. On the contrary, great good qualities are requisite to make amends for their having wealth, title, and office."

"There is a natural aristocracy among men. The grounds of this are virtue and talents. . . . There is also an artificial aristocracy founded on wealth and birth, without either virtue or talents; for with these it would belong to the first class. . . . The artificial aristocracy is a mischievous ingredient in government, and provision should be made to prevent its ascendency."

"A heavy aristocracy and corruption are two bridles in the mouths of [a people] which will prevent them from making any effectual efforts against their masters."

"To detail the real evils of aristocracy, they must be seen in Europe."

"Generally speaking, the proportion which the aggregate of the other classes of citizens bears in any state to that of its husbandmen is the proportion of its unsound to its healthy parts, and is a good enough barometer whereby to measure its degree of corruption."

"A due horror of the evils which flow from these distinctions [by birth or badge] could be excited in Europe only, where the dignity of man is lost in arbitrary distinctions, where the human species is classed into several stages of degradation, where the many are crushed under the weight of the few, and where the order established can present to the contemplation of a thinking being no other picture than that of God Almighty and His angels, trampling under foot the host of the damned."

"Lay down true principles and adhere to them inflexibly. Do not be frightened into their surrender by the alarms of the timid, or the croakings of wealth against the ascendency of the people."

Little could infuriate Jefferson more than the notion of governments that operate against the people:

"I am convinced that those societies (as the Indians) which live without government, enjoy in their general mass an infinitely greater degree of happiness than those who live under the European governments. Among the former, public opinion is in the place of law, and restrains morals as

powerfully as laws ever did anywhere.
Among the latter, under pretense of governing, they have divided their nations into
two classes, wolves and sheep. I do not
exaggerate. . . . Experience declares that
man is the only animal which devours his
own kind; for I can apply no milder term to
the governments of Europe, and to the general prey of the rich on the poor."

"The sheep are happier of themselves
than under the care of the wolves."

"[The European nations] are nations of
eternal war. All their energies are
expended in the destruction of the labor,
property and lives of their people. On our
part, never had a people so favorable a
chance of trying the opposite system, of
peace and fraternity with mankind, and the
direction of all our means and faculties to
the purpose of improvement instead of
destruction."

"How soon the labor of men would
make a paradise of the whole earth, were it
not for misgovernment, and a diversion of
all his energies from their proper object—
the happiness of man—to the selfish interest of kings, nobles, and priests."

Put simply, Jefferson believed that the
entire purpose of government is to enable
the people of a nation to live together in
safety, security, and happiness, and that
government exists for the interests of the
governed, not for the governors. As
Benjamin Franklin wrote, "In free governments the rulers are the servants and the
people their superiors and sovereigns."
Jefferson went even further:

"The whole body of the nation is the
sovereign legislative, judiciary, and executive power for itself. The inconvenience of
meeting to exercise these powers in person, and their inaptitude to exercise them,
induce them to appoint special organs to
declare their legislative will, to judge and
to execute it. It is the will of the nation
which makes the law obligatory; it is their
will which creates or annihilates the organ
which is to declare and announce it. They
may do it by a single person, as an emperor
of Russia (constituting his declarations evidence of their will), or by a few persons, as
the aristocracy of Venice, or by a complica-
tion of councils, as in our former regal government or our present republican one.
The law being law because it is the will of
the nation, is not changed by their chang-

ing the organ through which they choose to
announce their future will; no more than
the acts I have done by one attorney lose
their obligation by my changing or discon-
tinuing that attorney."

"Every nation has a right to govern itself
internally under what forms it pleases, and
to change these forms at its own will; and
externally to transact business with other
nations through whatever organ it chooses,
whether that be a King, Convention,
Assembly, Committee, President, or whatever it be. The only thing essential is, the
will of the nation."

"[The people] are in truth the only legitimate proprietors of the soil and government."

"The constitutions of most of our States
assert that all power is inherent in the people; that they may exercise it by themselves in all cases to which they think
themselves competent (as in electing their
functionaries executive and legislative, and
deciding by a jury of themselves in all judiciary cases in which any fact is involved),
or they may act by representatives, freely
and equally chosen; that it is their right

and duty to be at all times armed; that they are entitled to freedom of person, freedom of religion, freedom of property, and freedom of the press."

"We think experience has proved it safer for the mass of individuals composing the society to reserve to themselves personally the exercise of all rightful powers to which they are competent and to delegate those to which they are not competent to deputies named and removable for unfaithful conduct by themselves immediately."

"I consider the people who constitute a society or nation as the source of all authority in that nation; as free to transact their common concerns by any agents they think proper; to change these agents individually, or the organization of them in form or function whenever they please; that all the acts done by these agents under the authority of the nation are the acts of the nation, are obligatory on them . . . and can in no wise be annulled of affected by any change in the form of the government or of the persons administering it."

"When, by the Declaration of Independence, [the nation of Virginia] chose to abolish their former organs of declaring their will, the acts of will already formally and constitutionally declared, remained untouched. For the nation was not dissolved, was not annihilated; its will, therefore, remained in full vigor; and on the establishing the new organs, first of a convention, and afterwards a more complicated legislature, the old acts of national will continued in force, until the nation should, by its new organs, declare its will changed."

"Indeed in no case are the laws of a nation changed, of natural right, by their passage from one to another denomination. The soil, the inhabitants, their property, and the laws by which they are protected go together. Their laws are subject to be changed only in the case, and extent which their new legislature shall will."

"When a question arises, whether any particular law or appointment is still in force, we are to examine, not whether it was pronounced by the ancient or present organ, but whether it has been at any time revoked by the authority of the nation, expressed by the organ competent at the time."

"Necessities which dissolve a government do not convey its authority to an oligarchy or a monarchy. They throw back into the hands of the people the powers they had delegated, and leave them as individuals to shift for themselves."

"There is an error into which most of the speculators on government have fallen, and which the well-known state of society of our Indians ought, before now, to have corrected. In their hypothesis of the origin of government, they suppose it to have commenced in the patriarchal or monarchical form. Our Indians are evidently in that state of nature which has passed the association of a single family. . . . The Cherokees, the only tribe I know to be contemplating the establishment of regular laws, magistrates, and government, propose a government of representatives, elected from every town. But of all things, they least think of subjecting themselves to the will of one man."

"I consider the source of authority with us to be the Nation. Their will, declared through its proper organ, is valid till revoked by their will declared through its proper organ again also."

"What government [a nation] can bear depends not on the state of science, however exalted, in a select band of enlightened men, but on the condition of the general mind."

"The government of a nation may be usurped by the forcible intrusion of an individual into the throne. But to conquer its will so as to rest the right on that, the only legitimate basis, requires long acquiescence and cessation of all opposition."

"Independence can be trusted nowhere but with the people in mass. They are inherently independent of all but moral law."

"I have such reliance on the good sense of the body of the people and the honesty of their leaders that I am not afraid of their letting things go wrong to any length in any cause."

"Whenever our affairs go obviously wrong, the good sense of the people will interpose and set them to rights."

"Our fellow citizens have been led hoodwinked from their principles by a most

extraordinary combination of circumstances. But the band is removed, and they
now see for themselves."

"There is a steady, good sense in the
Legislature, and in the body of the nation,
joined with good intentions, which will
lead them to discern and to pursue the
public good under all circumstances which
can arise, and . . . no *ignis fatuus* [misleading
ideal] will be able to lead them long astray."

"I am sensible that there are defects in
our federal government, yet they are so
much lighter than those of monarchies,
that I view them with much indulgence. I
rely, too, on the good sense of the people
for remedy, whereas the evils of monarchical government are beyond remedy."

"My confidence is that there will for a
long time be virtue and good sense enough
in our countrymen to correct abuses."

"The force of public opinion cannot be
resisted when permitted freely to be
expressed. The agitation it produces must
be submitted to."

"A court has no affections; but those of
the people whom they govern influence

their decisions, even in the most arbitrary governments."

"Public opinion . . . [is] a censor before which the most exalted tremble for their future as well as present fame."

"When public opinion changes, it is with the rapidity of thought."

"Government being founded on opinion, the opinion of the public, even when it is wrong, ought to be respected to a certain degree."

"Opinions . . . constitute, indeed, moral facts, as important as physical ones to the attention of the public functionary."

"The people cannot be all, and always, well-informed. The part which is wrong will be discontented in proportion to the importance of the facts they misconceive. If they remain quiet under such misconceptions, it is a lethargy, the forerunner of death to the public liberty."

"I like to see the people awake and alert. The good sense of the people will soon lead them back if they have erred in a moment of surprise."

Few writers have gotten to the essence of the spirit of resistance with more eloquence than Jefferson:

"What country can preserve its liberties if its rulers are not warned from time to time that their people preserve the spirit of resistance? Let them take arms. The remedy is to set them right as to facts, pardon and pacify them."

"Governments, wherein the will of every one has a just influence . . . has its evils, . . . the principal of which is the turbulence to which it is subject. But weigh this against the oppressions of monarchy, and it becomes nothing. *Malo periculosam libertatem quam quietam servitutem.* [I prefer the tumult of liberty to the quiet of servitude.] Even this evil is productive of good. It prevents the degeneracy of government, and nourishes a general attention to the public affairs."

"The spirit of resistance to government is so valuable on certain occasions, that I wish it to be always kept alive. It will often be exercised when wrong, but better so than not to be exercised at all. I like a little rebellion now and then. It is like a storm in the atmosphere."

"Most codes extend their definitions of treason to acts not really against one's country. They do not distinguish between acts against the *government*, and acts against the *oppressions of the government*. The latter are virtues, yet have furnished more victims to the executioner than the former, because real treasons are rare; oppressions frequent. The unsuccessful strugglers against tyranny have been the chief martyrs of treason laws in all countries."

"The commotions that have taken place in America, as far as they are yet known to me, offer nothing threatening. They are a proof that the people have liberty enough, and I could not wish them less than they have. If the happiness of the mass of the people can be secured at the expense of a little tempest now and then, or even of a little blood, it will be a precious purchase. . . . Let common sense and common honesty have fair play, and they will soon set things to rights."

"The tumults in America I expected would have produced in Europe an unfavorable opinion of our political state. But it has not. On the contrary, the small effect of these tumults seems to have given more

confidence in the firmness of our governments. The interposition of the people
themselves on the side of government has
had a great effect on the opinion here [in
Europe]."

"The late rebellion in Massachusetts has
given more alarm than I think it should
have done. Calculate that one rebellion in
thirteen states in the course of eleven
years, is but one for each state in a century
and a half. No country should be so long
without one. Nor will any degree of power
in the hands of government prevent insurrections."

"Cherish . . . the spirit of our people,
and keep alive their attention. Do not be
too severe upon their errors, but reclaim
them by enlightening them."

"There are extraordinary situations
which require extraordinary interposition.
An exasperated people who feel that they
possess power are not easily restrained
within limits strictly regular."

"[The] uneasiness [of the people] has
produced acts absolutely unjustifiable; but I
hope they will provoke no severities from

their governments. A consciousness of those in power that their administration of the public affairs has been honest may, perhaps, produce too great a degree of indignation; and those characters wherein fear predominates over hope, may apprehend too much from these instances of irregularity. They may conclude too hastily, that nature has formed man insusceptible of any other government than that of force, a conclusion not founded in truth nor experience."

"I hold it that a little rebellion, now and then, is a good thing, and as necessary in the political world as storms are in the physical. Unsuccessful rebellions, indeed, generally establish the encroachments on the rights of the people, which have produced them. An observation of this truth should render honest republican governors so mild in their punishment of rebellions, as not to discourage them too much. It is medicine necessary for the sound health of government."

"[No] degree of power in the hands of government [will] prevent insurrections."

"The boisterous sea of liberty is never without a wave."

"What signify a few lives lost in a century or two? The tree of liberty must be refreshed from time to time with the blood of patriots and tyrants. It is its natural manure."

"Whenever any form of government becomes destructive of these ends [i.e., securing inherent and inalienable rights, with powers derived from the consent of the governed], it is the right of the people to alter or abolish it, and to institute new government, laying its foundation on such principles, and organizing its powers in such form, as to them shall seem most likely to effect their safety and happiness."

"In no country on earth is [a disposition to oppose the law by force] so impracticable as in one where every man feels a vital interest in maintaining the authority of the laws, and instantly engages in it as in his own personal cause."

"In a country whose constitution is derived from the will of the people directly expressed by their free suffrages, where the principal executive functionaries and those of the legislature are renewed by them at short periods, where under the character of jurors they exercise in person the greatest portion of the judiciary powers, where the laws are consequently so formed and administered as to bear with equal weight and favor on all, restraining no man in the pursuits of honest industry and securing to every one the property which that acquires, it would not be supposed that any safeguards could be needed against insurrection or enterprise on the public peace or authority. The laws, however, aware that these should not be trusted to moral restraints only, have wisely provided punishments for these crimes when committed."

"The paradox with me is how any friend to the union of our country can, in conscience, contribute a cent to the maintenance of anyone who perverts the sanctity of his desk to the open inculcation of rebellion, civil war, dissolution of government, and the miseries of anarchy."

"I acknowledge the right of voluntary associations for laudable purposes and in moderate numbers. I acknowledge, too, the expediency for revolutionary purposes of general associations coextensive with the nation. But where, as in our case, no

abuses call for revolution, voluntary associations so extensive as to grapple with and
control the government, should such be or
become their purpose, are dangerous
machines and should be frowned down in
every well regulated government."

"Private associations . . . whose magni-
tude may rivalize and jeopardize the march
of regular government [may become] necessary [in] the case where the regular
authorities of the government [combine]
against the rights of the people, and no
means of correction [remains] to them but
to organize a collateral power which, with
their support, might rescue and secure
their violated rights. But such is not the
case with our government. We need hazard
no collateral power which, by a change of
its original views and assumption of others
we know not how virtuous or how mischievous, would be ready organized and in
force sufficient to shake the established
foundations of society and endanger its
peace and the principles on which it is
based."

"Military assemblies will not only keep
alive the jealousies and fears of the civil
government, but give ground for these

fears and jealousies. For when men meet together, they will make business if they have none; they will collate their grievances, some real, some imaginary, all highly painted; they will communicate to each other the sparks of discontent; and these may engender a flame which will consume their particular, as well as the general happiness."

"Where an enterprise is meditated by private individuals against a foreign nation in amity with the United States, powers of prevention to a certain extent are given by the laws; would they not be as reasonable and useful were the enterprise preparing against the United States?"

"The framers of our constitution certainly supposed they had guarded, as well their government against destruction by treason, as their citizens against oppression under pretence of it; and if these ends are not attained, it is of importance to inquire by what means, more effectual, they may be secured."

"Looking forward with anxiety to [the] future destinies [of my fellow citizens], I trust that, in their steady character unshaken by difficulties, in their love of liberty, obedience to law, and support of the public authorities, I see a sure guaranty of the permanence of our republic."

"Democrats . . . consider the people as the safest depository of power in the last resort; they cherish them, therefore, and wish to leave in them all the powers to the exercise of which they are competent."

"The mass of the citizens is the safest depository of their own rights."

"I am not among those who fear the people. They, and not the rich, are our dependence for continued freedom."

"The people . . . are the only sure reliance for the preservation of our liberty."

"No government can continue good, but under the control of the people."

"Unless the mass retains sufficient control over those entrusted with the powers of their government, these will be perverted to their own oppression, and to the perpetuation of wealth and power in the individuals and their families selected for the trust."

"No other depositories of power [but the people themselves] have ever yet been found, which did not end in converting to their own profit the earnings of those committed to their charge."

"We fear that [violations of the Constitution] may produce insurrection. Nothing could be so fatal. Anything like force [used against the violators] would check the progress of the public opinion and rally them round the government. This is not the kind of opposition the American people will permit. But keep away all show of force and they will bear down the evil propensities of the government by the constitutional means of election and petition."

"Resort may be had to the people of the country, a more governable power from their principles and subordination; and rank and birth and tinsel-aristocracy will finally shrink into insignificance."

"The influence over government must be shared among all the people. If every individual which composes their mass participates of the ultimate authority, the government will be safe, because the corrupting [of] the whole mass will exceed any

private resources of wealth, and public
ones cannot be provided but by levies on
the people. In this case every man would
have to pay his own price."

"If once [the people] become inattentive
to the public affairs, you and I, and
Congress and Assemblies, Judges and
Governors, shall all become wolves. It
seems to be the law of our general nature,
in spite of individual exceptions."

"I know no safe depositary of the ultimate powers of the society but the people
themselves; and if we think them not
enlightened enough to exercise their control with a wholesome discretion, the remedy is not to take it from them, but to
inform their discretion by education. This
is the true corrective of abuses of constitutional power."

"The people, especially when moder-
ately instructed, are the only safe, because
the only honest, depositaries of the public
rights, and should therefore be introduced
into the administration of them in every
function to which they are sufficient; they
will err sometimes and accidentally, but
never designedly, and with a systematic

and persevering purpose of overthrowing the free principles of the government."

"There is one provision [in the new constitution of Spain] which will immortalize its inventors. It is that which, after a certain epoch, disfranchises every citizen who cannot read and write. This is new, and is the fruitful germ of the improvement of everything good and the correction of everything imperfect in the present constitution. This will give you an enlightened people, and an energetic public opinion which will control and enchain the aristocratic spirit of the government."

"Whenever the people are well-informed, they can be trusted with their own government. Whenever things get so far wrong as to attract their notice, they may be relied on to set them to rights."

"Above all things I hope the education of the common people will be attended to; convinced that on their good sense we may rely with the most security for the preservation of a due degree of liberty."

"Enlighten the people generally, and tyranny and oppressions of body and mind

will vanish like evil spirits at the dawn
of day."

"I am among those who think well of
the human character generally. I consider
man as formed for society and endowed by
nature with those dispositions which fit
him for society."

"Everyone, by his property or by his sat-
isfactory situation, is interested in the support of law and order. And such men may
safely and advantageously reserve to themselves a wholesome control over their public affairs and a degree of freedom which,
in the hands of the *canaille* of the cities of
Europe, would be instantly perverted to the
demolition and destruction of everything
public and private."

"Every man being at his ease feels an
interest in the preservation of order and
comes forth to preserve it at the first call of
the magistrate."

"The mobs of the great cities add just so
much to the support of pure government as
sores do to the strength of the human body.
It is the manners and spirit of a people
which preserve a republic in vigor. A degen-

eracy in these is a canker which soon eats to the heart of its laws and constitution."

"It was by the sober sense of our citizens that we were safely and steadily conducted from monarchy to republicanism, and it is by the same agency alone we can be kept from falling back."

"To the sincere spirit of republicanism are naturally associated the love of country, devotion to its liberty, its right and its honor."

"[It is the people's] conviction that a solid Union is the best rock of their safety."

"The cement of this Union is in the heart-blood of every American. I do not believe there is on earth a government established on so immovable a basis."

"Possessed of the blessing of self-government and of such a portion of civil liberty as no other civilized nation enjoys, it now behooves us to guard and preserve them by a continuance of the sacrifices and exertions by which they were acquired, and especially to nourish that Union which is their sole guarantee."

Jefferson strongly believed that the best form of government ever devised for protecting the rights of the people was the republican form. While imperfect, the form nevertheless gives people a voice and enables them to correct the course of government when they find it moving in the wrong direction.

"A democracy [is] the only pure republic, but impracticable beyond the limits of a town."

"Societies exist under three forms, sufficiently distinguishable. 1. Without government, as among our Indians. 2. Under governments, wherein the will of everyone has a just influence; as is the case in England, in a slight degree, and in our States, in a great one. 3. Under governments of force; as is the case in all other monarchies, and in most of the other republics. To have an idea of the curse of existence under these last, they must be seen. It is a government of wolves over sheep. It is a problem not clear in my mind that the first condition is not the best. But I believe it to be inconsistent with any great degree of population. The second state has a great deal of good in it. The mass of mankind under that,

enjoys a precious degree of liberty and happiness. It has its evils, too; the principal of
which is the turbulence to which it is subject. But weigh this against the oppressions
of monarchy, and it becomes nothing."

"The preeminence of representative
government [is maintained] by showing
that its foundations are laid in reason, in
right, and in general good."

"We may say with truth and meaning
that governments are more or less republican as they have more or less of the ele-
ment of popular election and control in
their composition; and believing as I do
that the mass of the citizens is the safest
depository of their own rights, and especially that the evils flowing from the
duperies of the people are less injurious
than those from the egoism of their agents,
I am a friend to that composition of government which has in it the most of this ingredient."

"The catholic principle of republicanism
[is] that every people may establish what
form of government they please and
change it as they please, the will of the
nation being the only thing essential."

"Independence of the will of the nation is a solecism, at least in a republican government."

"I freely admit the right of a nation to change its political principles and constitution at will."

"It accords with our principles to acknowledge any government to be rightful which is formed by the will of the nation substantially declared."

"Action by the citizens in person, in affairs within their reach and competence, and in all others by representatives, chosen immediately, and removable by themselves, constitutes the essence of a republic. . . . All governments are more or less republican in proportion as this principle enters more or less into their composition."

"Other shades of republicanism may be found in other forms of government, where the executive, judiciary, and legislative functions, and the different branches of the latter, are chosen by the people more or less directly, for longer terms of years, or for life, or made hereditary; or where there are mixtures of authorities, some dependent on, and others independent of the people."

"The hereditary branches of modern governments are the patrons of privilege and prerogative, and not of the natural rights of the people, whose oppressors they generally are."

"An hereditary aristocracy . . . will change the form of our governments from the best to the worst in the world. To know the mass of evil which flows from this fatal source, a person must be in France; he must see the finest soil, the finest climate, the most compact State, the most benevolent character of people, and every earthly advantage combined, insufficient to prevent this scourge from rendering existence a curse to twenty-four out of twenty-five parts of the inhabitants of this country."

"I was much an enemy of monarchies before I came to Europe. I am ten thousand times more so since I have seen what they are. There is scarcely an evil known in these countries which may not be traced to their king as its source, nor a good which is not derived from the small fibres of republicanism existing among them."

"Courts love the people always, as wolves do the sheep."

"The small and imperfect mixture of representative government in England, impeded as it is by other branches aristocratical and hereditary, shows yet the power of the representative principle towards improving the condition of man."

"The principles of government . . . [are] founded in the rights of man."

"The equality among our citizens [is] essential to the maintenance of republican government."

"No Englishman will pretend that a right to participate in government can be derived from any other source than a personal right, or a right of property."

"It is, indeed, of little consequence who governs us, if they sincerely and zealously cherish the principles of union and republicanism."

"From the moment that to preserve our rights a change of government became necessary, no doubt could be entertained that a republican form was most consonant with reason, with right, with the freedom of man, and with the character and situation of our fellow citizens."

"[To establish republican government, it is necessary to] effect a constitution in which the will of the nation shall have an organized control over the actions of its government, and its citizens a regular protection against its oppressions."

"[The first step is] to concur in a declaration of rights, at least, so that the nation may be acknowledged to have some fundamental rights not alterable by their ordinary legislature, and that this may form a ground work for future improvements."

"Where the citizens cannot meet to transact their business in person, they alone have the right to choose the agents who shall transact it; and . . . in this way a republican or popular government . . . may be exercised over any extent of country."

"I suspect that the doctrine, that small States alone are fitted to be republics, will be exploded by experience, with some other brilliant fallacies accredited by

Montesquieu and other political writers. Perhaps it will be found that to obtain a just republic (and it is to secure our just rights that we resort to government at all) it must be so extensive as that local egoisms may never reach its greater part; that on every particular question a majority may be found in its councils free from particular interests and giving, therefore, a uniform prevalence to the principles of justice. The smaller the societies, the more violent and more convulsive their schisms."

"It seems that the smaller the society the bitterer the dissensions into which it breaks. . . . I believe ours is to owe its permanence to its great extent, and the smaller portion comparatively which can ever be convulsed at one time by local passions."

"Our present federal limits are not too large for good government, nor will [an] increase of votes in Congress produce any ill effect. On the contrary, it will drown the little divisions at present existing there."

"The character which our fellow-citizens have displayed . . . gives us everything to hope for the permanence of our government. Its extent has saved us. While some parts were laboring under the paroxysm of delusion, others retained their senses, and time was thus given to the affected parts to recover their health."

"Every nation is liable to be under whatever bubble, design, or delusion may puff up in moments when off their guard."

"Montesquieu's doctrine that a republic can be preserved only in a small territory [has been proved a falsehood]. The reverse is the truth. Had our territory been even a third only of what it is we were gone. But while frenzy and delusion like an epidemic gained certain parts, the residue remained sound and untouched, and held on till their brethren could recover from the temporary delusion; and that circumstance has given me great comfort."

"I know that the acquisition of Louisiana has been disapproved by some, from a candid apprehension that the enlargement of our territory would endanger its union. But who can limit the extent to which the federative principle may operate effectively? The larger our association, the less will it be shaken by local passions."

"If ever this vast country is brought under a single government, it will be one of the most extensive corruption, indifferent and incapable of a wholesome care over so wide a spread of surface."

"I have much confidence that we shall proceed successfully for ages to come, and that, contrary to the principle of Montesquieu, it will be seen that the larger the extent of country, the more firm its republican structure, if founded, not on conquest, but in principles of compact and equality."

"My hope of [this country's] duration is built much on the enlargement of the resources of life going hand in hand with the enlargement of territory, and the belief that men are disposed to live honestly if the means of doing so are open to them."

Jefferson reflected long and hard on what he felt should be the proper size of states. He wrote to James Monroe in 1786:

"How may the territories of the Union be disposed of, so as to produce the greatest degree of happiness to their inhabitants? The ultramontane States . . . will not only be happier in States of moderate size, but it is the only way in which they can exist as a regular society. Considering the American character in general, that of those people particularly, and the energetic nature of our governments, a State of such extent as one hundred and sixty thousand square miles, would soon crumble into little ones. These are the circumstances which reduce the Indians to such small societies. They would produce an effect on our people similar to this. They would not be broken into such small pieces, because they are more habituated to subordination, and value more a government of regular law. But you would surely reverse the nature of things, in making small States on the ocean, and large ones beyond the mountains. If we could, in our consciences, say, that great States beyond the mountains will make the people happiest, we must still ask, whether they will be contented to be laid off into large States? They certainly will not; and, if they decide to divide themselves, we are not able to restrain them. They will end by separating from our confederacy, and becoming its enemies."

"A tractable people may be governed in large bodies; but, in proportion as they depart from this character, the extent of their government must be less. We see into what small divisions the Indians are obliged to reduce their societies."

"[If] we treat them [Indians] as fellow citizens, they will have a just share in their own government; they will love us, and pride themselves in an union with us. [If] we treat them as subjects, we govern them, and not they themselves; they will abhor us as masters, and break off from us in defiance."

"If, then, the control of the people over the organs of their government be the measure of its republicanism, and I confess I know no other measure, it must be agreed that our governments have much less of republicanism than ought to have been expected; in other words, that the people have less regular control over their agents, than their rights and their interests require. And this I ascribe, not to any want of republican dispositions in those who formed these constitutions, but to a submission of true principle to European authorities, to speculators on government, whose fears of the people have been inspired by the populace of their own great cities, and were unjustly entertained against the independent, the happy, and therefore orderly citizens of the United States. Much I apprehend that the golden moment is past for reforming these heresies. The functionaries of public power rarely strengthen in their dispositions to abridge it, and an unorganized call for timely amendment is not likely to prevail against an organized opposition to it."

"The great body of our native citizens are unquestionably of the republican sentiment. Foreign education, and foreign connections of interest, have produced some exceptions in every part of the Union, north and south, and perhaps other circumstances . . . may have thrown into the scale of exceptions a greater number of the rich. Still there, I believe, and here, I am sure, the great mass is republican. . . . Our countrymen left to the operation of their own unbiased good sense, I have no doubt we shall see . . . our citizens moving in phalanx in the paths of regular liberty, order, and a sacrosanct adherence to the Constitution."

"Our preference to [the republican] form of government has been so far justified by its success, and the prosperity with which it has blessed us. In no portion of the earth were life, liberty and property ever so securely held."

⁓

"I consider trial by jury as the only anchor ever yet imagined by man, by which a government can be held to the principles of its constitution."

"It is left . . . to the juries, if they think the permanent judges are under any bias whatever in any cause, to take on themselves to judge the law as well as the fact. They never exercise this power but when they suspect partiality in the judges; and by the exercise of this power they have been the firmest bulwarks of English liberty."

"If the question [before justices of the peace] relate to any point of public liberty, or if it be one of those in which the judges may be suspected of bias, the jury undertake to decide both law and fact."

"No provision in our Constitution ought to be dearer to man than that which protects the rights of conscience against the enterprises of the civil authority."

"The legislative powers of government reach actions only and not opinions."

"The liberty of speaking and writing guards our other liberties."

"[If a book were] very innocent, and one which might be confided to the reason of any man; not likely to be much read if let alone, but if persecuted, it will be generally read. Every man in the United States will think it a duty to buy a copy, in vindication of his right to buy and to read what he pleases."

"We are bound, you, I, and every one to make common cause, even with error itself, to maintain the common right of freedom of conscience."

"It behooves every man who values liberty of conscience for himself, to resist invasions of it in the case of others; or their case may, by change of circumstances, become his own. It behooves him, too, in his own case, to give no example of concession, betraying the common right of independent opinion, by answering questions of faith, which the laws have left between God and himself."

"The true foundation of republican government is the equal right of every citizen in his person and property and in their management."

"A right to property is founded in our natural wants, in the means with which we are endowed to satisfy these wants, and the right to what we acquire by those means without violating the similar rights of other sensible beings."

"The rights of the people to the exercise and fruits of their own industry can never be protected against the selfishness of rulers not subject to their control at short periods."

"To take from one because it is thought that his own industry and that of his father's has acquired too much, in order to spare to others, who, or whose fathers have not exercised equal industry and skill, is to violate arbitrarily the first principle of association—the guarantee to every one of a free exercise of his industry and the fruits acquired by it."

"Whenever there are in any country uncultivated lands and unemployed poor, it is clear that the laws of property have been so far extended as to violate natural right."

"By nature's law, every man has a right to seize and retake by force his own property taken from him by another, by force of fraud. Nor is this natural right among the first which is taken into the hands of regular government after it is instituted. It was long retained by our ancestors. It was a part of their common law, laid down in their books, recognized by all the authorities, and regulated as to circumstances of practice."

"It is a moot question whether the origin of any kind of property is derived from nature at all. It is agreed by those who have seriously considered the subject that no individual has, of natural right, a separate property in an acre of land, for instance. By a universal law, indeed, whatever, whether fixed or movable, belongs to all men equally and in common is the property for the moment of him who occupies it; but when he relinquishes the occupation, the property goes with it. Stable ownership is the gift of social law, and is given late in the progress of society."

"Private enterprise manages so much better all the concerns to which it is equal."

"The merchants will manage [commerce] the better, the more they are left free to manage for themselves."

On freedom of religion, Jefferson was equally adamantine:

"I consider the government of the United States as interdicted by the Constitution from intermeddling in religious institutions, their doctrines, discipline, or exercises."

"Religion is a subject on which I have ever been most scrupulously reserved. I have considered it as a matter between every man and his Maker, in which no other, and far less the public, had a right to intermeddle."

"The clergy, by getting themselves established by law, and ingrafted into the machine of government, have been a very formidable engine against the civil and religious rights of man."

"I am for freedom of religion, and against all maneuvers to bring about a legal ascendency of one sect over another."

"To compel a man to furnish contributions of money for the propagation of opinions which he disbelieves and abhors, is sinful and tyrannical."

"The clergy . . . believe that any portion of power confided to me [as President] will be exerted in opposition to their schemes. And they believe rightly: for I have sworn upon the altar of God, eternal hostility against every form of tyranny over the mind of man. But this is all they have to fear from me: and enough, too, in their opinion."

"Believing that religion is a matter which lies solely between man and his God, that he owes account to none other for his faith or his worship, that the legislative powers of government reach actions only, and not opinions, I contemplate with sovereign reverence that act of the whole American people which declared that their Legislature should 'make no law respecting an establishment of religion, or prohibiting the free exercise thereof,' thus building a wall of separation between Church and State."

"History, I believe, furnishes no example of a priest-ridden people maintaining a free civil government. This marks the lowest grade of ignorance of which their civil as well as religious leaders will always avail themselves for their own purposes."

"In every country and in every age, the priest has been hostile to liberty. He is always in alliance with the despot, abetting his abuses in return for protection to his own."

From Jefferson's first inaugural address in 1801:

"Having banished from our land that religious intolerance under which mankind so long bled and suffered, we have yet gained little if we countenance a political intolerance as despotic, as wicked, and capable of as bitter and bloody persecutions."

"The Christian religion, when divested of the rags in which they [the clergy] have enveloped it, and brought to the original purity and simplicity of its benevolent institutor, is a religion of all others most friendly to liberty, science, and the freest expansion of the human mind."

"Can the liberties of a nation be thought secure when we have removed their only firm basis, a conviction in the minds of the people that these liberties are of the gift of God?"

"Our particular principles of religion are a subject of accountability to God alone."

"Our civil rights have no dependence upon our religious opinions more than our opinions in physics or geometry."

"It is time enough, for the rightful purposes of civil government, for its officers to interfere [in the propagation of religious teachings] when principles break out into overt acts against peace and good order."

"No government can be maintained without the principle of fear as well as duty. Good men will obey the last, but bad ones the former only. If our government ever fails, it will be from this weakness."

"Every man is under the natural duty of contributing to the necessities of the society; and this is all the laws should enforce on him."

"A strict observation of the written laws is doubtless one of the high duties of a good citizen, but it is not the highest. The laws of necessity, of self-preservation, of saving our country when in danger, are of higher obligation. To lose our country by a scrupulous adherence to written law, would be to lose the law itself, with life, liberty, property, and all those who are enjoying them with us; thus absurdly sacrificing the end to the means."

"There is a debt of service due from every man to his country, proportioned to the bounties which nature and fortune have measured to him."

"I acknowledge that such a debt [of service to my fellow-citizens] exists, that a tour of duty in whatever line he can be most useful to his country, is due from every individual. It is not easy perhaps to say of what length exactly that tour should be, but we may safely say of what length it should not be. Not of our whole life, for instance, for that would be to be born a slave—not even of a very large portion of it."

"The man who loves his country on its own account, and not merely for its trappings of interest or power, can never be divorced from it, can never refuse to come forward when he finds that she is engaged in dangers which he has the means of warding off."

"It behooves our citizens to be on their guard, to be firm in their principles, and full of confidence in themselves. We are able to preserve our self-government if we will but think so."

"Lethargy is the forerunner of death to the public liberty."

"When a man assumes a public trust, he should consider himself as public property."

"The man who reads nothing at all is better educated than the man who reads nothing but newspapers."

And yet Jefferson felt as strongly about freedom of the press as he did about any other tenet of democracy:

"The basis of our governments being the opinion of the people, the very first object should be to keep that right; and were it left to me to decide whether we should have a government without newspapers or newspapers without a government, I should not hesitate a moment to prefer the latter."

"Our liberty cannot be guarded but by the freedom of the press, nor that be limited without danger of losing it."

"I am . . . for freedom of the press, and against all violations of the Constitution to silence by force and not by reason the complaints or criticisms, just or unjust, of our citizens against the conduct of their agents."

"The art of printing secures us against the retrogradation of reason and information."

"Considering the great importance to the public liberty of the freedom of the press, and the difficulty of submitting it to very precise rules, the laws have thought it less mischievous to give greater scope to its freedom than to the restraint of it."

"No experiment can be more interesting than that we are now trying, and which we trust will end in establishing the fact, that man may be governed by reason and truth. Our first object should therefore be, to leave open to him all the avenues to truth. The most effectual hitherto found, is the freedom of the press. It is, therefore, the first shut up by those who fear the investigation of their actions."

"This formidable censor of the public functionaries [the press], by arraigning them at the tribunal of public opinion, produces reform peaceably, which must otherwise be done by revolution. It is also the best instrument for enlightening the mind of man and improving him as a rational, moral, and social being."

"Our citizens may be deceived for awhile, and have been deceived; but as long as the presses can be protected, we may trust to them for light."

To Archibald Stuart, 1799: "The press is impotent when it abandons itself to falsehood."

"On the dogmas of religion, as distinguished from moral principles, all mankind, from the beginning of the world to this day, have been quarreling, fighting, burning and torturing one another for abstractions unintelligible to themselves and to all others, and absolutely beyond the comprehension of the human mind."

"Whenever a man has cast a longing eye on [holding public] offices, a rottenness begins in his conduct."

"Question with boldness even the existence of a God; because if there be one, he must more approve of the homage of reason than that of blindfolded fear."

"No man will ever bring out of the Presidency the reputation which carries him into it."

"We discover in the gospels a groundwork of vulgar ignorance, of things impossible, of superstition, fanaticism and fabrication."

"Christianity neither is, nor ever was, a part of the common law."

"I live for books."

"No laborious person was ever yet hysterical."

"The price of freedom is eternal vigilance."

"Were we to act but in cases where no contrary opinion of a lawyer can be had, we should never act."

"Delay is preferable to error."

"When angry, count ten before you speak; if very angry, a hundred."

"The spirit of resistance to government is so valuable on certain occasions that I wish it to be always kept alive."

"Is uniformity attainable? Millions of innocent men, women, and children, since the introduction of Christianity, have been burnt, tortured, fined, imprisoned; yet we have not advanced one inch towards uniformity. What has been the effect of coercion? To make one half the world fools, and the other half hypocrites. To support roguery and error all over the earth."

After his first inauguration, an admirer asked permission to congratulate Jefferson. "I would advise you to follow my example on nuptial occasions," replied the new president, "when I always tell the bride-groom I will wait till the end of the year before offering my congratulations."

"On the dogmas of religion, as distin-guished from moral principles, all mankind, from the beginning of the world to this day, have been quarreling, fighting, burning and torturing one another, for abstractions unintelligible to themselves and to all others, and absolutely beyond the comprehension of the human mind."

Baptists were not part of the Congregationalist establishment, and some were experiencing serious persecution. The Danbury (Connecticut) Baptist Association, concerned about religious lib-erty in the new nation, wrote to President Thomas Jefferson:

OCT. 7, 1801.

Sir,
Among the many millions in America and Europe who rejoice in your Election to office; we embrace the

first opportunity which we have
enjoyed in our collective capacity,
since your Inauguration, to express our
great satisfaction, in your appointment
to the chief Majestracy in the United
States; And though our mode of expression may be less courtly and pompous
than what many others clothe their
addresses with, we beg you, Sir to
believe, that none are more sincere.

Our Sentiments are uniformly on
the side of Religious Liberty—That
Religion is at all times and places a matter between God and individuals—That
no man ought to suffer in name, person,
or effects on account of his religious
Opinions—That the legitimate Power of
civil government extends no further
than to punish the man who works *ill to
his neighbor*: But Sir our constitution of
government is not specific. Our ancient
charter together with the Laws made
coincident therewith, were adopted on
the Basis of our government, at the time
of our revolution; and such had been
our Laws & usages, and such still are;
that Religion is considered as the first
object of Legislation; and therefore
what religious privileges we enjoy (as a
minor part of the State) we enjoy as

favors granted, and not as inalienable
rights: and these favors we receive at
the expense of such degrading acknowl-
edgements, as are inconsistent with the
rights of freemen. It is not to be won-
dered at therefore; if those, who seek
after power & gain under the pretense
of *government & Religion* should
reproach their fellow men—should
reproach their chief Magistrate, as an
enemy of religion Law & good order
because he will not, dare not assume
the prerogatives of Jehovah and make
Laws to govern the Kingdom of Christ.

Sir, we are sensible that the
President of the United States is not the
national legislator, and also sensible that
the national government cannot destroy
the Laws of each State; but our hopes
are strong that the sentiments of our
beloved President, which have had such
genial affect already, like the radiant
beams of the Sun, will shine and prevail
through all these States and all the
world till Hierarchy and Tyranny be
destroyed from the Earth. Sir, when we
reflect on your past services, and see a
glow of philanthropy and good will shin-
ing forth in a course of more than thirty
years we have reason to believe that

America's God has raised you up to fill
the chair of State out of that good will
which he bears to the Millions which
you preside over. May God strengthen
you for the arduous task which providence & the voice of the people have
cald you to sustain and support you in
your Administration against all the predetermined opposition of those who
wish to rise to wealth & importance on
the poverty and subjection of the people.
And may the Lord preserve you safe
from every evil and bring you at last to
his Heavenly Kingdom through Jesus
Christ our Glorious Mediator.

> SIGNED IN BEHALF OF THE
> ASSOCIATION.
> NEH DODGE
> EPHRAM ROBBINS
> THE COMMITTEE
> STEPHEN S. NELSON

Jefferson's Answer to the Danbury
Baptists:

JANUARY 1, 1802

Gentlemen:
The affectionate sentiments of
esteem and approbation which are so
good to express towards me, on behalf

of the Danbury Baptist Association,
give me the highest satisfaction. My
duties dictate a faithful and zealous
pursuit of the interests of my constituents, and in proportion as they are
persuaded of my fidelity to those
duties, the discharge of them becomes
more and more pleasing.

Believing with you that religion is
a matter which lies solely between
man and his God; that he owes account
to none other for his faith or his worship; that the legislative powers of the
government reach actions only, and not
opinions, I contemplate with sovereign
reverence that act of the whole
American people which declared that
their legislature should "make no law
respecting an establishment of religion, or prohibiting the free exercise
thereof," thus building a wall of separation between church and State.
Adhering to this expression of the
supreme will of the nation in behalf of
the rights of conscience, I shall see
with sincere satisfaction the progress
of those sentiments which tend to
restore man to all of his natural rights,
convinced he has no natural right in
opposition to his social duties.

I reciprocate your kind prayers for the protection and blessings of the common Father and Creator of man, and tender you and your religious association, assurances of my high respect and esteem.

THOMAS JEFFERSON

"No free man shall ever be debarred the use of arms. The strongest reason for the people to retain the right to keep and bear arms is, as a last resort, to protect themselves against tyranny in government."

"We have not so far perfected our constitutions as to venture to make them unchangeable. . . . But can they be made unchangeable? . . . I think not. . . . Nothing then is unchangeable but the inherent and unalienable rights of man."

While he was ambassador to France, a friend's daughter asked Jefferson to procure a few corsets for her. His response: "Mr. Jefferson has the honor to present to Mrs. Smith and to send her the two pair of Corsets she desired. He wishes they may be suitable, as Mrs. Smith omitted to send her measure. . . . [S]hould they be too small, however, she will be so good as to lay them by a while. There are ebbs as well as flows in this world. When the mountain refused to come to Mahomet, he went to the mountain."

"The man who fears no truths has nothing to fear from lies."

"It is error alone which needs the support of government. Truth can stand by itself."

"The legitimate powers of government extend to such acts only as are injurious to others. But it does me no injury for my neighbor to say there are twenty gods, or no god. It neither picks my pocket nor breaks my leg."

"I have sworn upon the altar of Almighty God eternal hostility against every form of tyranny over the mind of man."

Jefferson on the future of democracy:

"I am entirely persuaded that the agitations of the public mind advance its powers, and that at every vibration between the points of liberty and despotism, something will be gained for the former. As men become better informed, their rulers must respect them the more."

"The people of every country are the only safe guardians of their own rights, and are the only instruments which can be used for their destruction. And certainly they would never consent to be so used were they not deceived. To avoid this they should be instructed to a certain degree."

"The most effectual means of preventing the perversion of power into tyranny are to illuminate, as far as practicable, the minds of the people at large, and more especially to give them knowledge of those facts which history exhibits, that possessed thereby of the experience of other ages and countries, they may be enabled to know ambition under all its shapes, and prompt to exert their natural powers to defeat its purposes."

"Time indeed changes manners and notions, and so far we must expect institutions to bend to them. But time produces also corruption of principles, and against this it is the duty of good citizens to be ever on the watch, and if the gangrene is to prevail at last, let the day be kept off as long as possible."

"The time to guard against corruption and tyranny is before they shall have gotten hold of us. It is better to keep the wolf out of the fold, than to trust to drawing his teeth and talons after he shall have entered."

"The general spread of the light of science has already laid open to every view the palpable truth that the mass of mankind has not been born with saddles on their backs nor a favored few booted and spurred, ready to ride them legitimately by the grace of God."

"A single good government becomes . . . a blessing to the whole earth, its welcome to the oppressed restraining within certain limits the measure of their oppressions. But should even this be counteracted by violence on the right of expatriation, the other branch of our example then presents itself for imitation: to rise on their rulers and do as we have done."

"A first attempt to recover the right of self government may fail, so may a second, a third, etc. But as a younger and more instructed race comes on, the sentiment becomes more and more intuitive, and a fourth, a fifth, or some subsequent one of the ever renewed attempts will ultimately succeed. . . . To attain all this, however, rivers of blood must yet flow, and years of desolation pass over; yet the object is worth rivers of blood and years of desolation. For what inheritance so valuable can man leave to his posterity?"

"A government regulating itself by what is wise and just for the many, uninfluenced by the local and selfish views of the few who direct their affairs, has not been seen, perhaps, on earth. Or if it existed for a moment at the birth of ours, it would not be easy to fix the term of its continuance. Still, I believe it does exist here in a greater degree than anywhere else; and for its growth and continuance . . . I offer sincere prayers."

"May [our Declaration of Independence] be to the world, what I believe it will be (to some parts sooner, to others later, but finally to all), the signal of arousing men to burst the chains under which monkish ignorance and superstition had persuaded them to bind themselves, and to assume the blessings and security of self-government. . . . All eyes are opened, or opening, to the rights of man."

"The flames kindled on the Fourth of July, 1776, have spread over too much of the globe to be extinguished by the feeble engines of despotism; on the contrary, they will consume these engines and all who work them."

Late in life, Jefferson compared romance to a young colt: "It must be broken before it is safe to ride."

"That government governs best that governs least."

James Madison

(1751–1836)

Fourth President of the United States

"The purpose of separation of church
and state is to keep forever from these
shores the ceaseless strife that has soaked
the soil of Europe in blood for centuries."

"As the instrument came from them it
was nothing more than the draft of a plan,

nothing but a dead letter, until life and valid-
ity were breathed into it by the voice of the
people, speaking through the several state
conventions. If we were to look, therefore,
for the meaning of the instrument beyond
the face of the instrument, we must look for
it, not in the general convention, which proposed, but in the state conventions, which
accepted and ratified the Constitution."

"What is government itself but the
greatest of all reflections on human nature?
If men were angels, no government would
be necessary. If angels were to govern men,
neither external nor internal controls on
government would be necessary."

"A certain degree of preparation for war
. . . affords also the best security for the continuance of peace."

"No government any more than an individual will long be respected without being
truly respectable."

"There are more instances of the
abridgement of the freedom of the people
by gradual and silent encroachments of
those in power than by violent and sudden
usurpations."

"It is vain to say that enlightened states-men will always be able to adjust their interests. Enlightened men will not always be at the helm."

"Respect for character is always dimin-ished in proportion to the number among whom the blame or praise is to be divided."

"The President is responsible to the public for the conduct of the person he has nominated and appointed."

"Religious bondage shackles and debili-tates the mind and unfits it for every noble enterprise, every expanded prospect."

"Who does not see that the same author-ity which can establish Christianity in exclusion of all other religions may estab-lish, with the same ease, any particular sect of Christians in exclusion to all other sects?"

"In the Papal System, Government and religion are in a manner consolidated, and that is found to be the worst of Gov-ernment."

"Ecclesiastical establishments tend to great ignorance and corruption, all of which facilitate the execution of mischievous projects."

"What influence in fact have ecclesiastical establishments had on civil society? In some instances they have been seen to erect a spiritual tyranny on the ruins of civil authority; in many instances they have been seen upholding the thrones of political tyranny; in no instances have they been seen the guardians of the liberties of the people."

"During almost fifteen centuries has the legal establishment of Christianity been on trial. What has been its fruits? More or less in all places, pride and indolence in the clergy; ignorance and servility in the laity; in both, superstition, bigotry, and persecution."

"Every man who loves peace, every man who loves his country, every man who loves liberty ought to have it ever before his eyes that he may cherish in his heart a due attachment to the Union of America and be able to set a due value on the means of preserving it."

"The most productive system of finance will always be the least burdensome."

"It becomes all therefore who are
friends of a Government based on free
principles to reflect, that by denying the
possibility of a system partly federal and
partly consolidated, and who would convert
ours into one either wholly federal or
wholly consolidated, in neither of which
forms have individual rights, public order,
and external safety, been all duly maintained, they aim a deadly blow at the last
hope of true liberty on the face of the
Earth."

"The powers delegated by the proposed
Constitution to the federal government are
few and defined. Those which are to
remain in the State governments are
numerous and indefinite."

"Such an institution may be sometimes
necessary as a defense to the people
against their own temporary errors and
delusions."

"If we resort for a criterion to the different principles on which different forms of
government are established, we may define
a republic to be, or at least may bestow that
name on, a government which derives all
its powers directly or indirectly from the

great body of the people, and is administered by persons holding their offices during pleasure for a limited period, or during
good behavior."

"A dependence on the people is, no
doubt, the primary control on the government; but experience has taught mankind
the necessity of auxiliary precautions."

"The belief in a God All Powerful wise
and good, is so essential to the moral
order of the world and to the happiness of
man, that arguments which enforce it cannot be drawn from too many sources nor
adapted with too much solicitude to the
different characters and capacities
impressed with it."

"We have heard of the impious doctrine
in the old world, that the people were made
for kings, not kings for the people. Is the
same doctrine to be revived in the new, in
another shape that the solid happiness of
the people is to be sacrificed to the views of
political institutions of a different form? It
is too early for politicians to presume on
our forgetting that the public good, the real
welfare of the great body of the people, is
the supreme object to be pursued; and that

no form of government whatever has any other value than as it may be fitted for the attainment of this object."

"That diabolical Hell conceived principle of persecution rages among some and to their eternal Infamy the Clergy can furnish their Quota of Imps for such business."

"It is the duty of every man to render to the Creator such homage, and such only, as he believes to be acceptable to him. This duty is precedent both in order of time and degree of obligation, to the claims of Civil Society. Before any man can be considered as a member of Civil Society, he must be considered as a subject of the Governor of the Universe."

"It is the duty of every man to render to the Creator such homage and such only as he believes to be acceptable to him. This duty is precedent, both in order of time and in degree of obligation, to the claims of Civil Society."

"There is no maxim in my opinion which is more liable to be misapplied, and which therefore needs elucidation than the current one that the interest of the majority is the political standard of right and wrong. . . . In fact it is only reestablishing under another name and a more specious form, force as the measure of right. . . ."

On slavery:

"[The Convention] thought it wrong to admit in the Constitution the idea that there could be property in men."

"We have seen the mere distinction of color made in the most enlightened period of time, a ground of the most oppressive dominion ever exercised by man over man."

"All men having power ought to be distrusted to a certain degree."

"As long as the reason of man continues fallible, and he is at liberty to exercise it, different opinions will be formed. As long as the connection subsists between his reason and his self-love, his opinions and his passions will have a reciprocal influence on each other."

"The diversity in the faculties of men from which the rights of property originate, is not less an insuperable obstacle to a uniformity of interests. The protection of these faculties is the first object of government."

"The great security against a gradual concentration of the several powers in the same department consists in giving to those who administer each department the necessary constitutional means and personal motives to resist encroachment of the others."

"The apportionment of taxes on the various descriptions of property is an act which seems to require the most exact impartiality; yet there is, perhaps, no legislative act in which greater opportunity and temptation are given to a predominant party to trample on the rules of justice. Every shilling which they overburden the inferior number is a shilling saved to their own pockets."

"Among the numerous advantages promised by a well-constructed Union, none deserves to be more accurately developed than its tendency to break and control the violence of faction."

"Democracies have ever been spectacles of turbulence and contention; have ever been found incompatible with personal security, or the rights of property; and have, in general, been as short in their lives as they have been violent in their deaths."

"The latent causes of faction are thus sown in the nature of man."

"They accomplished a revolution which has no parallel in the annals of human society. They reared the fabrics of governments which have no model on the face of the globe. They formed the design of a great Confederacy, which it is incumbent on their successors to improve and perpetuate."

"In the first place, it is to be remembered, that the general government is not to be charged with the whole power of making and administering laws: its jurisdiction is limited to certain enumerated objects, which concern all the members of the republic, but which are not to be attained by the separate provisions of any."

"Is it not the glory of the people of America, that whilst they have paid a decent regard to the opinions of former times and other nations, they have not suffered a blind veneration for antiquity, for custom, or for names, to overrule the suggestions of their own good sense, the knowledge of their own situation, and the lessons of their own experience? To this manly spirit, posterity will be indebted for the possession, and the world for the example of the numerous innovations displayed on the American theatre, in favor of private rights and public happiness."

"America united with a handful of troops, or without a single soldier, exhibits a more forbidding posture to foreign ambition than America disunited, with a hundred thousand veterans ready for combat."

"The great desideratum in Government is, so to modify the sovereignty as that it may be sufficiently neutral between different parts of the Society to control one part from invading the rights of another, and at the same time sufficiently controlled itself, from setting up an interest adverse to that of the entire Society."

"In forming the Senate, the great anchor of the Government, the questions as they came within the first object turned mostly on the mode of appointment, and the duration of it."

"An elective despotism was not the government we fought for; but one in which the powers of government should be so divided and balanced among the several bodies of magistracy as that no one could transcend their legal limits without being effectually checked and restrained by the others."

"For the same reason that the members of the State legislatures will be unlikely to attach themselves sufficiently to national objects, the members of the federal legislature will be likely to attach themselves too much to local objects."

"Besides the advantage of being armed, which the Americans possess over the people of almost every other nation, the existence of subordinate governments, to which the people are attached and by which the militia officers are appointed, forms a barrier against the enterprises of ambition, more insurmountable than any which a simple government of any form can admit of."

"No political truth is certainly of greater intrinsic value, or is stamped with the authority of more enlightened patrons of liberty than that on which the objection is founded. The accumulation of all powers, legislative, executive, and judiciary, in the same hands, whether of one, a few, or many, and whether hereditary, self-appointed, or elective, may justly be pronounced the very definition of tyranny."

"In the next place, to show that unless these departments be so far connected and blended as to give to each a constitutional control over the others, the degree of separation which the maxim requires, as essential to a free government, can never in practice be duly maintained."

"The legislative department is everywhere extending the sphere of its activity and drawing all power into its impetuous vortex."

"One hundred and seventy-three despots would surely be as oppressive as one."

"It will not be denied that power is of an encroaching nature and that it ought to be effectually restrained from passing the limits assigned to it. After discriminating, therefore, in theory, the several classes of power, as they may in their nature be legislative, executive, or judiciary, the next and most difficult task is to provide some practical security for each, against the invasion of the others."

"As there is a degree of depravity in mankind which requires a certain degree of circumspection and distrust: So there are other qualities in human nature, which justify a certain portion of esteem and confidence. Republican government presupposes the existence of these qualities in a higher degree than any other form. Were the pictures which have been drawn by the political jealousy of some among us, faithful likenesses of the human character, the inference would be that there is not sufficient virtue among men for self-government; and that nothing less than the chains of despotism can restrain them from destroying and devouring one another."

"Had every Athenian citizen been a Socrates, every Athenian assembly would still have been a mob."

"Such will be the relation between the House of Representatives and their constituents. Duty, gratitude, interest, ambition itself, are the cords by which they will be bound to fidelity and sympathy with the great mass of the people."

"If it be asked what is to restrain the House of Representatives from making legal discriminations in favor of themselves and a particular class of the society? I answer, the genius of the whole system, the nature of just and constitutional laws, and above all the vigilant and manly spirit which actuates the people of America, a spirit which nourishes freedom, and in return is nourished by it."

"The house of representatives . . . can make no law which will not have its full operation on themselves and their friends, as well as the great mass of society. This has always been deemed one of the strongest bonds by which human policy can connect the rulers and the people together. It creates between them that communion of interest, and sympathy of sentiments, of which few governments have furnished examples; but without which every government degenerates into tyranny."

"The aim of every political constitution is, or ought to be, first to obtain for rulers men who possess most wisdom to discern, and most virtue to pursue, the common good of the society; and in the next place, to take the most effectual precautions for keeping them virtuous whilst they continue to hold their public trust."

"The members of the legislative department . . . are numerous. They are distributed and dwell among the people at large. Their connections of blood, of friendship, and of acquaintance embrace a great proportion of the most influential part of the society. . . . [T]hey are more immediately the confidential guardians of their rights and liberties."

"It is the reason alone, of the public, that ought to control and regulate the government."

"It may be considered as an objection inherent in the principle, that as every appeal to the people would carry an implication of some defect in the government, frequent appeals would in great measure deprive the government of that veneration which time bestows on everything, and without which perhaps the wisest and freest governments would not possess the requisite stability."

"The passions, therefore, not the reason, of the public would sit in judgment. But it is the reason, alone, of the public, that ought to control and regulate the government. The passions ought to be controlled and regulated by the government."

"If men were angels, no government would be necessary. If angels were to govern men, neither external nor internal controls on government would be necessary. In framing a government which is to be administered by men over men, the great difficulty lies in this: you must first enable the government to control the governed; and in the next place, oblige it to control itself."

"In a society under the forms of which the stronger faction can readily unite and oppress the weaker, anarchy may as truly be said to reign as in a state of nature."

"Ambition must be made to counteract ambition. The interest of the man must be connected with the constitutional rights of the place. It may be a reflection on human nature that such devices should be necessary to control the abuses of government."

"Justice is the end of government. It is the end of civil society. It ever has been and ever will be pursued until it be obtained, or until liberty be lost in the pursuit."

"It is impossible for the man of pious reflection not to perceive in [the Constitution] a finger of that Almighty hand which has been so frequently and signally extended to our relief in the critical stages of the revolution."

"Energy in government is essential to that security against external and internal danger and to that prompt and salutary execution of the laws which enter into the very definition of good government. Stability in government is essential to national character and to the advantages annexed to it, as well as to that repose and confidence in the minds of the people, which are among the chief blessings of civil society."

"But the mild voice of reason, pleading the cause of an enlarged and permanent

interest, is but too often drowned, before
public bodies as well as individuals, by the
clamors of an impatient avidity for immediate and immoderate gain."

"What is to be the consequence, in case
the Congress shall misconstrue this part
[the necessary and proper clause] of the
Constitution and exercise powers not war-
ranted by its true meaning, I answer the
same as if they should misconstrue or
enlarge any other power vested in them. . . .
[T]he success of the usurpation will depend
on the executive and judiciary departments, which are to expound and give
effect to the legislative acts; and in a last
resort a remedy must be obtained from the
people, who can by the elections of more
faithful representatives, annul the acts of
the usurpers."

"A local spirit will infallibly prevail
much more in the members of Congress
than a national spirit will prevail in the legislatures of the particular States."

"Is there no virtue among us? If there be
not, we are in a wretched situation. No the-
oretical checks—no form of government
can render us secure. To suppose that any

form of government will secure liberty or happiness without any virtue in the people, is a chimerical idea, if there be sufficient virtue and intelligence in the community, it will be exercised in the selection of these men. So that we do not depend on their virtue, or put confidence in our rulers, but in the people who are to choose them."

"Refusing or not refusing to execute a law to stamp it with its final character . . . makes the Judiciary department paramount in fact to the Legislature, which was never intended and can never be proper."

"The invasion of private rights is chiefly to be apprehended, not from acts of Government contrary to the sense of its constituents, but from acts in which the Government is the mere instrument of the major number of the Constituents."

"Wherever the real power in a Government lies, there is the danger of oppression."

"The civil rights of none, shall be abridged on account of religious belief or worship, nor shall any national religion be established, nor shall the full and equal rights of conscience be in any manner, or on any pretext infringed."

"I acknowledge, in the ordinary course of government, that the exposition of the laws and Constitution devolves upon the judicial. But I beg to know upon what principle it can be contended that any one department draws from the Constitution greater powers than another in marking out the limits of the powers of the several departments."

"Nothing has yet been offered to invalidate the doctrine that the meaning of the Constitution may as well be ascertained by the Legislative as by the Judicial authority."

"If individuals be not influenced by moral principles; it is in vain to look for public virtue; it is, therefore, the duty of legislators to enforce, both by precept and example, the utility, as well as the necessity of a strict adherence to the rules of distributive justice."

"There is not a more important and fundamental principle in legislation, than that the ways and means ought always to face the public engagements; that our appropriations

should ever go hand in hand with our promises. To say that the United States should be
answerable for twenty-five millions of dollars
without knowing whether the ways and
means can be provided, and without knowing whether those who are to succeed us will
think with us on the subject, would be rash
and unjustifiable. Sir, in my opinion, it would
be hazarding the public faith in a manner
contrary to every idea of prudence."

"A republic, by which I mean a government in which the scheme of representation
takes place, opens a different prospect and
promises the cure for which we are seeking."

"Nothing is so contagious as opinion,
especially on questions which, being sus-
ceptible of very different glosses, beget in
the mind a distrust of itself."

"Public opinion sets bounds to every
government, and is the real sovereign in
every free one."

"A universal peace, it is to be feared, is
in the catalogue of events, which will never
exist but in the imaginations of visionary
philosophers, or in the breasts of benevolent enthusiasts."

"In Europe, charters of liberty have been granted by power. America has set the example . . . of charters of power granted by liberty. This revolution in the practice of the world, may, with an honest praise, be pronounced the most triumphant epoch of its history, and the most consoling presage of its happiness."

"If Congress can do whatever in their discretion can be done by money, and will promote the General Welfare, the Government is no longer a limited one, possessing enumerated powers, but an indefinite one, subject to particular exceptions."

"Where an excess of power prevails, property of no sort is duly respected. No man is safe in his opinions, his person, his faculties, or his possessions."

"As a man is said to have a right to his property, he may be equally said to have a property in his rights. Where an excess of power prevails, property of no sort is duly respected. No man is safe in his opinions, his person, his faculties, or his possessions."

"Conscience is the most sacred of all property."

"A just security to property is not afforded by that government, under which unequal taxes oppress one species of property and reward another species."

"Government is instituted to protect property of every sort; as well that which lies in the various rights of individuals, as that which the term particularly expresses. This being the end of government, that alone is a just government which impartially secures to every man whatever is his own."

"The government of the United States is a definite government, confined to specified objects. It is not like the state governments, whose powers are more general. Charity is no part of the legislative duty of the government."

"To the press alone, checkered as it is with abuses, the world is indebted for all the triumphs which have been gained by reason and humanity over error and oppression."

"The right of freely examining public characters and measures, and of free communication among the people thereon . . .

has ever been justly deemed the only effectual guardian of every other right."

"To render the justice of the war on our part the more conspicuous, the reluctance to commence it was followed by the earliest and strongest manifestations of a disposition to arrest its progress. The sword was scarcely out of the scabbard before the enemy was apprised of the reasonable terms on which it would be re-sheathed."

"To exclude foreign intrigues and foreign partialities, so degrading to all countries and so baneful to free ones; to foster a spirit of independence too just to invade the rights of others, too proud to surrender our own, too liberal to indulge unworthy prejudices ourselves and too elevated not to look down upon them in others; to hold the union of the States on the basis of their peace and happiness; to support the Constitution, which is the cement of the Union, as well in its limitations as in its authorities; to respect the rights and authorities reserved to the States and to the people as equally incorporated with and essential to the success of the general . . . as far as sentiments and intentions such as these can aid the fulfillment of my duty, they will be a resource which can not fail me."

"It is a principle incorporated into the settled policy of America, that as peace is better than war, war is better than tribute."

"Equal laws protecting equal rights . . . the best guarantee of loyalty and love of country."

"Among the features peculiar to the political system of the United States, is the perfect equality of rights which it secures to every religious sect."

"A popular Government, without popular information, or the means of acquiring it, is but a Prologue to a Farce or a Tragedy; or, perhaps both. Knowledge will forever govern ignorance: And a people who mean to be their own Governors, must arm themselves with the power which knowledge gives."

"What spectacle can be more edifying or more seasonable, than that of Liberty and Learning, each leaning on the other for their mutual & surest support?"

"We are teaching the world the great truth that Governments do better without Kings & Nobles than with them. The merit will be doubled by the other lesson that Religion Flourishes in greater purity, without than with the aid of Government."

"The eyes of the world being thus on our Country, it is put the more on its good behavior, and under the greater obligation also, to do justice to the Tree of Liberty by an exhibition of the fine fruits we gather from it."

"I entirely concur in the propriety of resorting to the sense in which the Constitution was accepted and ratified by the nation. In that sense alone it is the legitimate Constitution. And if that is not the guide in expounding it, there may be no security for a consistent and stable, more than for a faithful exercise of its powers. If the meaning of the text be sought in the changeable meaning of the words composing it, it is evident that the shape and attributes of the Government must partake of the changes to which the words and phrases of all living languages are constantly subject. What a metamorphosis would be produced in the code of law if all its ancient phraseology were to be taken in its modern sense. And that the language of our Constitution is already undergoing interpretations unknown to its founder, will I believe appear to all unbiassed Enquirers into the history of its origin and adoption."

"On the distinctive principles of the Government . . . of the U. States, the best guides are to be found in . . . The Declaration of Independence, as the fundamental Act of Union of these States."

"The best service that can be rendered to a Country, next to that of giving it liberty, is in diffusing the mental improvement equally essential to the preservation, and the enjoyment of the blessing."

"The essence of Government is power; and power, lodged as it must be in human hands, will ever be liable to abuse."

"It is sufficiently obvious, that persons and property are the two great subjects on which Governments are to act; and that the rights of persons, and the rights of property, are the objects, for the protection of which Government was insti-

tuted. These rights cannot well be separated."

"It is due to justice; due to humanity;
due to truth; to the sympathies of our
nature; in fine, to our character as a people,
both abroad and at home, that they should
be considered, as much as possible, in the
light of human beings, and not as mere
property. As such, they are acted upon by
our laws, and have an interest in our laws."

"It has been said that all Government is
an evil. It would be more proper to say that
the necessity of any Government is a misfortune. This necessity however exists; and
the problem to be solved is, not what form
of Government is perfect, but which of the
forms is least imperfect."

"You give me a credit to which I have no
claim in calling me 'the writer of the
Constitution of the United States.' This was
not, like the fabled Goddess of Wisdom, the
offspring of a single brain. It ought to be
regarded as the work of many heads and
many hands."

"Whatever may be the judgment pronounced on the competency of the architects

of the Constitution, or whatever may be the destiny of the edifice prepared by them, I feel it a duty to express my profound and solemn conviction . . . that there never was an assembly of men, charged with a great and arduous trust, who were more pure in their motives, or more exclusively or anxiously devoted to the object committed to them."

In his final years, Madison came to be fêted as the Father of the Constitution. He took this in stride: "Having outlived so many of my contemporaries, I ought not to forget that I may be thought to have outlived myself."

On his deathbed, Madison's niece asked him what was wrong. His dying words:

"Nothing more than a change of mind, my dear."

Alexander Hamilton

(1755–1804)

American Statesman

"The best we can hope for concerning the people at large is that they be properly armed."

"The idea of restraining the legislative authority in the means of providing for the national defense is one of those refinements which owe their origin to a

zeal for liberty more ardent than enlightened."

"When occasions present themselves, in
which the interests of the people are at
variance with their inclinations, it is the
duty of the persons whom they have
appointed to be the guardians of those
interests, to withstand the temporary delusion, in order to give them time and opportunity for more cool and sedate reflection."

"It is a singular advantage of taxes on
articles of consumption that they contain in
their own nature a security against excess.
They prescribe their own limit, which cannot be exceeded without defeating the end
purposed—that is, an extension of the revenue."

"To grant that there is a supreme intelligence who rules the world and has established laws to regulate the actions of his
creatures; and still to assert that man, in a
state of nature, may be considered as perfectly free from all restraints of law and
government, appears to a common under-
standing altogether irreconcilable. Good
and wise men, in all ages, have embraced a
very dissimilar theory. They have supposed

that the deity, from the relations we stand
in to himself and to each other, has consti-
tuted an eternal and immutable law, which
is indispensably obligatory upon all
mankind, prior to any human institution
whatever. This is what is called the law of
nature. . . . Upon this law depend the natural rights of mankind."

"Why has government been instituted at
all? Because the passions of men will not
conform to the dictates of reason and justice without constraint."

"The citizens of America have too much
discernment to be argued into anarchy, and
I am much mistaken if experience has not
wrought a deep and solemn conviction in
the public mind that greater energy of government is essential to the welfare and
prosperity of the community."

"No man in his senses can hesitate in
choosing to be free, rather than a slave."

"The sacred rights of mankind are not
to be rummaged for, among old parch-
ments, or musty records. They are written, as with a sunbeam, in the whole volume of human nature, by the hand of the

divinity itself; and can never be erased or obscured by mortal power."

"The fundamental source of all your errors, sophisms and false reasonings is a total ignorance of the natural rights of mankind. Were you once to become acquainted with these, you could never entertain a thought, that all men are not, by nature, entitled to a parity of privileges. You would be convinced, that natural liberty is a gift of the beneficent Creator to the whole human race, and that civil liberty is founded in that; and cannot be wrested from any people, without the most manifest violation of justice."

"There is a certain enthusiasm in liberty, that makes human nature rise above itself, in acts of bravery and heroism."

"A fondness for power is implanted, in most men, and it is natural to abuse it, when acquired."

"The fabric of American empire ought to rest on the solid basis of the consent of the people. The streams of national power ought to flow from that pure, original fountain of all legitimate authority."

"The circumstances that endanger the safety of nations are infinite, and for this reason no constitutional shackles can wisely be imposed on the power to which the care of it is committed."

"Wise politicians will be cautious about fettering the government with restrictions that cannot be observed, because they know that every break of the fundamental laws, though dictated by necessity, impairs that sacred reverence which ought to be maintained in the breast of rulers towards the constitution of a country."

"The prosperity of commerce is now perceived and acknowledged by all enlightened statesmen to be the most useful as well as the most productive source of national wealth, and has accordingly become a primary object of its political cares."

"Of those men who have overturned the liberties of republics, the greatest number have begun their career by paying an obsequious court to the people, commencing demagogues and ending tyrants."

"It seems to have been reserved to the people of this country, by their conduct and example, to decide the important question, whether societies of men are really capable or not of establishing good government from reflection and choice, or whether they are forever destined to depend for their political constitutions on accident and force. If there be any truth in the remark, the crisis at which we are arrived may with propriety be regarded as the era in which that decision is to be made; and a wrong election of the part we shall act may, in this view, deserve to be considered as the general misfortune of mankind."

"In politics, as in religion, it is equally absurd to aim at making proselytes by fire and sword. Heresies in either can rarely be cured by persecution."

"The truth is, after all the declamations we have heard, that the Constitution is itself, in every rational sense, and to every useful purpose, a bill of rights."

"The standard of good behavior for the continuance in office of the judicial magistracy is certainly one of the most valuable of the modern improvements in the practice of government."

"And it proves, in the last place, that liberty can have nothing to fear from the judiciary alone, but would have everything to fear from its union with either of the other departments."

"In the first place, there is not a syllable in the plan under consideration which directly empowers the national courts to construe the laws according to the spirit of the Constitution, or which gives them any greater latitude in this respect than may be claimed by the courts of every State."

"The Judiciary . . . has no influence over either the sword or the purse; no direction either of the strength or of the wealth of the society, and can take no active resolution whatever. It may truly be said to have neither force nor will."

"There is not a syllable in the plan under consideration which directly empowers the national courts to construe the laws according to the spirit of the Constitution."

"The true principle of government is this—make the system compleat in its structure; give a perfect proportion and balance to its parts; and the powers you give it will never affect your security."

"It was remarked yesterday that a numerous representation was necessary to obtain the confidence of the people. This is not generally true. The confidence of the people will easily be gained by a good administration. This is the true touchstone."

"The Constitution ought to be the standard of construction for the laws, and that wherever there is an evident opposition, the laws ought to give place to the Constitution. But this doctrine is not deducible from any circumstance peculiar to the plan of convention, but from the general theory of a limited Constitution."

"In disquisitions of every kind there are certain primary truths, or first principles, upon which all subsequent reasoning must depend."

"If a well-regulated militia be the most natural defense of a free country, it ought certainly to be under the regulation and at

the disposal of that body which is consti-
tuted the guardian of the national security.
If standing armies are dangerous to liberty, an efficacious power over the militia
in the same body ought, as far as possible,
to take away the inducement and the pretext to such unfriendly institutions. If the
federal government can command the aid
of the militia in those emergencies which
call for the military arm in support of the
civil magistrate, it can the better dispense
with the employment of a different kind of
force. If it cannot avail itself of the former,
it will be obliged to recur to the latter. To
render an army unnecessary will be a
more certain method of preventing its
existence than a thousand prohibitions
upon paper."

"There is something so far-fetched and
so extravagant in the idea of danger to liberty from the militia that one is at a loss
whether to treat it with gravity or with
raillery; whether to consider it as a mere
trial of skill, like the paradoxes of rhetori-
cians; as a disingenuous artifice to instil
prejudices at any price; or as the serious."

"To judge from the history of mankind,
we shall be compelled to conclude that the

fiery and destructive passions of war reign in the human breast with much more powerful sway than the mild and beneficent sentiments of peace; and that to model our political systems upon speculations of lasting tranquillity would be to calculate on the weaker springs of human character."

"The great leading objects of the federal government, in which revenue is concerned, are to maintain domestic peace, and provide for the common defense. In these are comprehended the regulation of commerce that is, the whole system of foreign intercourse; the support of armies and navies, and of the civil administration."

"I trust that the proposed Constitution afford a genuine specimen of representative government and republican government; and that it will answer, in an eminent degree, all the beneficial purposes of society."

"The history of ancient and modern republics had taught them that many of the evils which those republics suffered arose from the want of a certain balance, and that mutual control indispensable to a wise administration. They were convinced that

popular assemblies are frequently mis-
guided by ignorance, by sudden impulses,
and the intrigues of ambitious men; and
that some firm barrier against these operations was necessary. They, therefore, instituted your Senate."

"The great desiderata are a free representation and mutual checks. When these
are obtained, all our apprehensions of the
extent of powers are unjust and imaginary."

"As riches increase and accumulate in
few hands, as luxury prevails in society,
virtue will be in a greater degree considered as only a graceful appendage of
wealth, and the tendency of things will be
to depart from the republican standard.
This is the real disposition of human
nature; it is what neither the honorable
member nor myself can correct. It is a
common misfortunate that awaits our State
constitution, as well as all others."

"I will venture to assert that no combination of designing men under heaven
will be capable of making a government
unpopular which is in its principles a wise
and good one, and vigorous in its operations."

"It is an unquestionable truth, that the body of the people in every country desire sincerely its prosperity. But it is equally unquestionable that they do not possess the discernment and stability necessary for systematic government. To deny that they are frequently led into the grossest of errors, by misinformation and passion, would be a flattery which their own good sense must despise."

"I am persuaded that a firm union is as necessary to perpetuate our liberties as it is to make us respectable; and experience will probably prove that the National Government will be as natural a guardian of our freedom as the State Legislatures."

"When you assemble from your several counties in the Legislature, were every member to be guided only by the apparent interest of his county, government would be impracticable. There must be a perpetual accommodation and sacrifice of local advantage to general expediency."

"There are certain social principles in human nature, from which we may draw the most solid conclusions with respect to the conduct of individuals and of communities. We love our families more than our neighbors; we love our neighbors more than our countrymen in general. The human affections, like solar heat, lose their intensity as they depart from the centre. . . . On these principles, the attachment of the individual will be first and for ever secured by the State governments. They will be a mutual protection and support."

"The local interest of a State ought in every case to give way to the interests of the Union. For when a sacrifice of one or the other is necessary, the former becomes only an apparent, partial interest, and should yield, on the principle that the smaller good ought never to oppose the greater good."

"This balance between the National and State governments ought to be dwelt on with peculiar attention, as it is of the utmost importance. It forms a double security to the people. If one encroaches on their rights they will find a powerful protection in the other. Indeed, they will both be prevented from overpassing their constitutional limits by a certain rivalship, which will ever subsist between them."

"The State governments possess inherent advantages, which will ever give them an influence and ascendancy over the National Government, and will for ever preclude the possibility of federal encroachments. That their liberties, indeed, can be subverted by the federal head, is repugnant to every rule of political calculation."

"While the constitution continues to be read, and its principles known, the states, must, by every rational man, be considered as essential component parts of the union; and therefore the idea of sacrificing the former to the latter is totally inadmissible."

"Good constitutions are formed upon a comparison of the liberty of the individual with the strength of government: If the tone of either be too high, the other will be weakened too much. It is the happiest possible mode of conciliating these objects, to institute one branch peculiarly endowed with sensibility, another with knowledge and firmness. Through the opposition and mutual control of these bodies, the government will reach, in its regular operations, the perfect balance between liberty and power."

"This process of election affords a moral certainty that the office of President will seldom fall to the lot of any man who is not in an eminent degree endowed with the requisite qualifications."

"A feeble executive implies a feeble execution of the government. A feeble execution is but another phrase for a bad execution; and a government ill-executed, whatever may be its theory, must be, in practice, a bad government."

"Energy in the executive is a leading character in the definition of good government. It is essential to the protection of the community against foreign attacks; it is not less essential to the steady administration of the laws; to the protection of property against those irregular and high-handed combinations which sometimes interrupt the ordinary course of justice; to the security of liberty against the enterprises and assaults of ambition, of faction, and of anarchy."

"It is a just observation that the people commonly intend the Public Good. This often applies to their very errors. But their good sense would despise the adulator who should pretend they always reason right about the means of promoting it."

"The republican principle demands that the deliberate sense of the community should govern the conduct of those to whom they entrust the management of their affairs; but it does not require an unqualified complaisance to every sudden breeze of passion or to every transient impulse which the people may receive from the arts of men, who flatter their prejudices to betray their interests."

"If mankind were to resolve to agree in no institution of government, until every part of it had been adjusted to the most exact standard of perfection, society would soon become a general scene of anarchy, and the world a desert."

"The tendency of a national bank is to increase public and private credit. The former gives power to the state, for the protection of its rights and interests: and the latter facilitates and extends the operations of commerce among individuals. Industry is increased, commodities are multiplied, agriculture and manufacturers flourish: and herein consists the true wealth and prosperity of a state."

"However weak our country may be, I hope we shall never sacrifice our liberties."

"As on the one hand, the necessity for borrowing in particular emergencies cannot be doubted, so on the other, it is equally evident that to be able to borrow upon good terms, it is essential that the credit of a nation should be well established."

"States, like individuals, who observe their engagements, are respected and trusted: while the reverse is the fate of those who pursue an opposite conduct."

"To cherish and stimulate the activity of the human mind, by multiplying the objects of enterprise, is not among the least considerable of the expedients, by which the wealth of a nation may be promoted."

"Measures which serve to abridge the free competition of foreign Articles, have a tendency to occasion an enhancement of prices."

"Wherever indeed a right of property is infringed for the general good, if the nature of the case admits of compensation, it ought to be made; but if compensation be impracticable, that impracticability ought to

be an obstacle to a clearly essential
reform."

"Foreign influence is truly the Grecian
horse to a republic. We cannot be too care-
ful to exclude its influence."

"If it be asked, What is the most sacred
duty and the greatest source of our security
in a Republic? The answer would be, An
inviolable respect for the Constitution and
Laws—the first growing out of the last. . . .
A sacred respect for the constitutional law
is the vital principle, the sustaining energy
of a free government."

"The instrument by which it [govern-
ment] must act are either the authority of
the laws or force. If the first be destroyed,
the last must be substituted; and where this
becomes the ordinary instrument of government there is an end to liberty!"

"As to Taxes, they are evidently inseparable from Government. It is impossible
without them to pay the debts of the nation,
to protect it from foreign danger, or to
secure individuals from lawless violence
and rapine."

"The present Constitution is the standard to which we are to cling. Under its banners, bona fide must we combat our political foes—rejecting all changes but through the channel itself provides for amendments."

Alexander Hamilton was killed in a famous duel with Aaron Burr, whose political aspirations Hamilton had repeatedly thwarted. In a letter to his wife, Elizabeth (Eliza) Schuyler, penned before the duel, he wrote, "the scruples of a Christian have determined me to expose my own life to any extent rather than subject myself to the guilt of taking the life of another." He felt so strongly about this that he reiterated the sentiment with his dying words to her:

"Remember, my Eliza, you are a Christian."

BENJAMIN RUSH

(1745–1813)

Physician, Professor, Author, Treasurer of the U.S. Mint, and Signator of the Declaration of Independence

"Patriotism is as much a virtue as justice, and is as necessary for the support of societies as natural affection is for the support of families."

"Without religion, I believe that learning does real mischief to the morals and principles of mankind."

"The American war is over; but this far from being the case with the American revolution. On the contrary, nothing but the first act of the drama is closed. It remains yet to establish and perfect our new forms of government, and to prepare the principles, morals, and manners of our citizens for these forms of government after they are established and brought to perfection."

"Where there is no law, there is no liberty; and nothing deserves the name of law but that which is certain and universal in its operation upon all the members of the community."

"The only foundation for a useful education in a republic is to be laid in religion. Without this there can be no virtue, and without virtue there can be no liberty, and liberty is the object and life of all republican governments."

"In such a performance you may lay the foundation of national happiness only in religion, not by leaving it doubtful 'whether morals can exist without it,' but by asserting that without religion morals are the effects of causes as purely physical as pleasant breezes and fruitful seasons."

"Some talked, some wrote, and some fought to promote and establish it, but you [John Adams] and Mr. Jefferson thought for us all. I never take a retrospect of the years 1775 and 1776 without associating your opinions and speeches and conversations with all the great political, moral, and intellectual achievements of the Congress of those memorable years."

"[Poets] view the human mind in all its operations, whether natural or morbid, with a microscopic eye, and hence many things arrest their attention, which escape the notice of physicians."

"If there were no hereafter, individuals and societies would be great gainers by attending public worship every Sunday. Rest from labor in the house of God winds up the machine of both soul and body better than anything else, and thereby invigorates it for the labors and duties of the ensuing week."

In 1793, yellow fever struck Philadelphia for the first time in thirty-one years. The disease totally baffled even the most skilled physicians in town. Dr. Rush wrote about the calamity:

"This general calamity lasted for about one hundred days, extending from July till November. The deaths in the whole of this distressing period, were four thousand and forty-four, or something more than thirty-eight each day, on an average. Whole families were confined by it. There was a great deficiency of nurses for the sick. There was likewise a great deficiency of physicians, from the desertion of some, and the sickness and death of others. At one time, there were but three physicians, who were able to do business out of their houses, and at this time there were probably not less than six thousand persons ill with the fever.

"A cheerful countenance was scarcely to be seen for six weeks. The streets everywhere discovered marks of the distress that pervaded the city. In walking for many hundred yards, few persons were met, except such as were in quest of a physician, a nurse, a bleeder, or the men who buried the dead. The hearse alone kept up the remembrance of the noise of carriages, or carts, in the streets. A black man leading or driving a horse, with a corpse, on a pair of chair wheels, met the eye in most of the streets of the city, at every hour of the day; while the noise of the same wheels passing slowly over the pavement kept alive anguish and fear in the sick and well, every hour of the night."

Dr. Rush pored over every bit of medical literature he could get his hands on to find out everything he could about yellow fever. One book recommended the use of a powerful evacuant such as calomel. Dr. Rush tried the remedy, purging his patients and bleeding them lightly, and to his great jubilation, it worked. He entered in his notebook:

"Thank God, out of one hundred patients whom I have visited or prescribed for this day, I have lost none."

He later wrote: "Many whole families, consisting of five, six, and, in three instances, of nine members, were recovered by plentiful purging and bleeding. These remedies were prescribed with great advantage by several of the physicians of the city. But the use of them was not restricted to the physicians alone; the clergy, the apothecaries, many private citizens, several intelligent women, and two black men, prescribed them with great success. Nay, more, many persons prescribed them to themselves. It was owing to the almost universal use of these remedies, that the mortality of the disease diminished in proportion as the number of persons who were affected by it increased. It is probable that not less than six thousand of the inhabitants of Philadelphia were saved from death by bleeding and purging; during the autumn of 1793."

Dr. Rush was a deeply devout man:

In 1830, he wrote an essay defending the use of the Bible in public schools. It read, in part:

"I know there is an objection among many people to teaching children doctrines of any kind, because they are liable to be controverted. But let us not be wiser than our Maker. If moral precepts alone could have reformed mankind, the mission of the Son of God into our world would have

been unnecessary. He came to promulgate
a system of doctrines, as well as a system
of morals. The perfect morality of the
Gospel rests upon a doctrine which,
though often controverted, has never been
refuted; I mean the vicarious life and death
of the Son of God. This sublime and ineffa-
ble doctrine delivers us from the absurd
hypothesis of modern philosophers concerning the foundation of moral obligation,
and fixes it upon the eternal and self-mov-
ing principle of LOVE. It concentrates a
whole system of ethics in a single text of
Scripture: 'A new commandment I give
unto you, that ye love one another, even as
I have loved you.' By withholding the
knowledge of this doctrine from children,
we deprive ourselves of the best means of
awakening moral sensibility in their
minds. We do more; we furnish an argument for withholding from them a knowledge of the morality of the Gospel likewise;
for this, in many instances, is as supernat-
ural, and therefore as liable to be controverted, as any of the doctrines or miracles
which are mentioned in the New
Testament. The miraculous conception of
the Saviour of the world by a virgin is not
more opposed to the ordinary course of
natural events, nor is the doctrine of the

atonement more above human reason,
than those moral precepts which command
us to love our enemies or to die for our
friends."

When the Constitution was ratified with
Rush as one of the signators, he wrote to a
friend on July 9, 1788:

"'Tis done. We have become a nation."

THOMAS PAINE

(1737–1809)

Politician, Philosopher, and Author

"These are the times that try men's souls. The summer soldier and the sunshine patriot, will, in this crisis, shrink from the service of their country; but he that stands it now deserves the love and thanks of man and woman."

"Tyranny, like hell, is not easily con-
quered; yet we have this consolation with
us, that the harder the conflict, the more
glorious the triumph."

"The sublime and the ridiculous are
often so nearly related, that it is difficult to
class them separately. One step above the
sublime makes the ridiculous, and one step
above the ridiculous makes the sublime
again."

"Independence is my happiness, and I
view things as they are, without regard to
place or person; my country is the world,
and my religion is to do good."

"The trade of governing has always
been monopolized by the most ignorant
and the most rascally individuals of
mankind."

"Some writers have so confounded society with government, as to leave little or
no distinction between them; whereas they
are not only different, but have different
origins. Society is produced by our wants,
and government by our wickedness; the
former promotes our happiness positively
by uniting our affections, the latter nega-
tively by restraining our vices. The one

encourages intercourse, the other creates distinctions. The first is a patron, the last a punisher."

"The most formidable weapon against errors of every kind is reason. I have never used any other, and I trust I never shall."

"My mind is my own church."

"All national institutions of churches, whether Jewish, Christian, or Turkish, appear to me no other than human inventions set up to terrify and enslave mankind, and monopolize power and profit."

"Age after age has passed away, for no other purpose than to behold their wretchedness."

"Reason and Ignorance, the opposites of each other, influence the great bulk of mankind. If either of these can be rendered sufficiently extensive in a country, the machinery of Government goes easily on. Reason obeys itself; and Ignorance submits to whatever is dictated to it."

"Any system of religion that has anything in it that shocks the mind of a child cannot be a true system."

"The danger to which the success of revolutions is most exposed, is that of attempting them before the principles on which they proceed, and the advantages to result from them, are sufficiently seen and understood."

"Of all the tyrannies that affect mankind, tyranny in religion is the worst."

"When men yield up the privilege of thinking, the last shadow of liberty quits the horizon."

"Practical religion consists in doing good: and the only way of serving God is that of endeavoring to make His creation happy. All preaching that has not this for its object is nonsense and hypocrisy."

"He who dares not offend cannot be honest."

"When shall it be said in any country of the world, my poor are happy; neither ignorance or distress is to be found among them; my jails are empty of prisoners, my streets of beggars; the aged are not in want, the taxes are not oppressive; the rational world is my friend, because I am the friend of its happiness; when these things can be said, then may that country boast of its constitution and government."

"Time makes more converts than reason."

"Society in every state is a blessing, but government, even in its best state is but a necessary evil; in its worst state an intolerable one."

"The cause of America is in a great measure the cause of all mankind. Where, say some, is the king of America? I'll tell you friend, He reigns from above."

"Those who expect to reap the blessings of freedom must, like men, undergo the fatigue of supporting it."

"A long habit of not thinking a thing wrong, gives it a superficial appearance of being right."

"The harder the conflict, the more glorious the triumph. What we obtain too cheap, we esteem too lightly; it is dearness only that gives everything its value. I love the man that can smile in trouble, that can gather strength from distress and grow brave by reflection. 'Tis the business of little minds to shrink; but he whose heart is firm, and whose conscience approves his conduct, will pursue his principles unto death."

"He that would make his own liberty secure must guard even his enemy from oppression; for if he violates this duty he establishes a precedent that will reach to himself."

"The trade of government has always been monopolized by the most ignorant and the most rascally individuals of mankind."

"The age of ignorance commenced with the Christian system."

"Belief in a cruel God makes a cruel man."

"Let them call me a rebel and I welcome it. I feel no concern from it; but I should suffer the misery of demons were I to make a whore of my soul."

INDEX